Rebel's One-of-a-Kind Miracle Blood

A Novel by Paul Murdock

Introduction

Five-year-old Mark Barker from the novel, "*What a Guy!!*", is now eighteen. In that novel, he was transfused with blood from the now-deceased half-wolf-and-half-German-Shepherd, "Rebel", by a top-secret scientist at Lake Louise.

The young lad inherited bipolar disorder and schizophrenia from his biological parents. The miracle news is that the blood from the deceased animal contains a substance that will cure both disorders. This substance greatly improves the quality of life and is called "*Rebel's One-of-a-Kind Miracle Blood.*"

Rihanna Valentine, an animal breeder, created Rebel by cross-breeding his German Shepherd father with a wolf mother. Rihanna ends up at the hospital as a patient.

Meanwhile, Mark has to track down Robert Ryder who first appeared in a previous novel, "*What a Guy!!*", before his mind is destroyed.

Both of them will become part of an experiment to test the Miracle Blood before it will be deemed safe to transfuse into other patients.

Robert had suffered from schizophrenia during his days of university. Rihanna was never diagnosed with bipolar disorder until she flipped out on her hospital hairdresser employee, Aunt Bubble from the novels, "*What a Guy!!*", and "*Lonely Memories*". She had been admitted into the hospital by the hospital security staff.

The old drug that Robert was taking to control his disorders was discontinued by the drug company when two new drugs were discovered that provided a better quality of life for sufferers of bipolar disorder and schizophrenia. When Robert was switched to one of these new drugs it triggered hallucinations and Robert went missing.

One of Robert's friends notified his older brother, Dave Ryder, an RCMP member from *"What a Guy!!"*, that Robert was missing and he ordered a search for his rescue.

The Heavenly Creator has chosen Rebel, who was the longest and healthiest living half-wolf-and-half-German-shepherd, and blessed him with the powerful blood.

Mark learns the truth that he is adopted and has had Rebel's one-of-a-kind miracle blood transfusion.

How is he going to react to it? Will he accept it? Read along and find out!

Chapter one

In the early summer sunrise, on the quiet Lake Louise road, the only vehicle was an ambulance. The driver, paramedic Simon Barker is dressed in his uniform and wearing blue sunglasses. He turns on the radio and is surprised to hear:

"Good morning, Mr. Simon Barker! My name is 'Rebel'. I am an angel sent by the Heavenly Creator. You can see me in your mirror, running next to you."

Simon looked in the left mirror and saw a black German Shepherd catching up to him. He smiled and honked twice at the speeding dog to say, "Hello!"

Then Simon heard another voice on the radio, "Hi! My name is also 'Rebel'. I too am an angel sent by the Heavenly Creator. You can see me running with the first angel."

Again, Simon looked in the mirror and this time he saw a white wolf with blue eyes running next to the black German Shepherd. Again, he honked twice to say "Hello!"

The black German Shepherd said, "My mission is to deal with your son, Mark Barker. See you at the cottage!"

The white wolf said, "My mission is to guard a young missing man named Robert Ryder. See you in the woods."

Then the two speeding animals went separate directions.

Simon smiled as he continued driving. He turned the music on after the two animals left on their own individual journeys.

...

The black German Shepherd trotted down the side of the highway. The weather was warm and the traffic was light with couples and families travelling for vacations...

The black German Shepherd hitched a ride on the back of a truck, enjoying the fresh air...

The black German Shepherd got off the truck at the coffee shop, crossed the park where children were playing on slides and merry-go-rounds and swinging on swings with their parents watching...

The black German Shepherd stopped at the beach where people were covering their skin with shiny lotion and wearing sunglasses. Many were lying on towels in the sun. Children were building sandcastles. People of all ages and a flock of quacking ducks were swimming along...

Away from the swimmers was an abandoned wooden raft. The black German Shepherd was curious enough to check it out. He jumped on the raft. But the raft wasn't tied to the dock and it started drifting down the coast, carrying the dog past every dock and cottage along the shore...

Chapter Two

At their cottage, Shaunabell Barker, a swimming instructor, and Rihanna Valentine, an animal breeder and hairdresser were having a conversation while three mixed-breed German Shepherd / Collies were training to become lifeguard assistants in the water near the beach.

"Elaine Williams is the name of the swimming instructor who trained me to do this for a living," said Shaunabell.

"Elaine Williams?" said Rihanna. "That was the teen girl who rescued her sister from drowning in the Pacific Ocean several years ago, according to the news."

"I remember hearing about it," said Shaunabell. "That brave girl sounded so characteristic, according to her interview."

"Actually, I know her and her family from Edmonton personally," said Rihanna.

"How did you…?" asked Shaunabell.

"Her mother responded to my ad when I was looking for customers to buy my dogs," said Rihanna.

"Small world!" They both said, laughing.

…

Tasha Toddler arrived to take her three dogs home for the day. "Hi, Shaunabell and Rihanna! How are my dogs coming along in their training?"

"Awesome!" said Shaunabell. "All of them are doing remarkably well, so they'll be qualified to become lifeguard assistants pretty soon!"

"Oh, I'm so proud of them," said Tasha.

"It is my privilege," said Shaunabell.

"And you, Rihanna?" said Tasha, holding her hand with a friendly smile. "How did the fur shaving go? Any problems?"

"Two of them of were no problem," said Rihanna. "But it took quite a while for one of them to trust me. It was her first shaving so I sang her a song."

Rihanna started singing in a high-pitched voice that was deafening, loud enough to hurt the owner's ears, and Shaunabell's, too.

"Whoa!" Tasha was stunned. "I've never heard anyone who could sing in such high-pitched tone before! It sounds like somebody is super happy."

Rihanna felt embarrassed and tried to avoid further conversation. "Actually, it's time for me to go home."

"Oh, Rihanna," said Tasha. "I am also here to pay you the bill for shaving their fur. How much does it cost, again?"

"The same as the last bill," said Rihanna.

The owner took out her cell phone and e-transferred the payment. Almost immediately, Rihanna received the notice on her cell phone, so she signed on and deposited the payment in her business account.

"Thank you,"

"You're welcome."

"Bye," Rihanna quickly walked away still feeling embarrassed.

"Bye," said the Tasha.

Tasha spent a couple of minutes chatting with Shaunabell about how Rihanna responded and her concern about Rihanna's singing behaviour. Then she loaded her family of three pets in the back of her truck and headed home.

. . .

Seconds later, Mark Barker, Shaunabell's son, showed up with a black German Shepherd.

"Who's dog is that?" asked Shaunabell. "Where does he come from?"

"I discovered him on a raft that came floating out of nowhere when I was swimming," said Mark.

Mark tried to take the dog into the water but the animal backed away, barking once. Shaunabell noticed something about the frightened dog.

"Oh, Mark, don't force him," said Shaunabell. "He probably has some sort of phobia, a water phobia, I figure. How about you take him into the cottage? Tell dad about how you discovered the dog. I'll give him swimming instructions later, but right now, I'm waiting for my other clients to show up. I'll see you later in the evening."

"OK, mom," said Mark. "See you when I come home from work."

Mark brought his new pet into the kitchen, just as Simon Barker arrived home from work, still wearing his paramedic uniform and sunglasses.

"High, dad!" said Mark as he ran up to him, greeting him with a bear hug.

"Hi there, my big boy!" said Simon wrapping his muscular arms around his son.

"Look what I found!" said Mark, pointing to the dog standing next to him. "His name is, uh — Buddy! He's my new Buddy! Mom told me to tell you that she'll be Buddy's swimming instructor. She thinks he has a water phobia just by the way he was behaving when I discovered him on a floating wooden raft. How about I feed him something?"

Simon looked at his watch. "You're going to be late for work, Mark, so you better get going! I'll feed your little angel."

"My little angel?" asked Mark, confused. "What do you mean he's my—"

"Never mind! Just move your butt and go!" Simon insisted with firmness.

Mark quickly changed into his work uniform and left for work.

Chapter Three

Mark was a hard-working fulltime waiter at a family restaurant. He dealt with a lot of customers with different personalities. The head chef, Joseph, was very impressed with Mark for his good nature and how appropriately he treated his customers with their complaints. Mark respected everyone's privacy without asking any questions, unless it was work-related.

Mark earned top wages and excellent tips. All his hard-earned income was to go toward his first year in university to study medicine. His goal was to become a psychiatrist.

His favourite customer was Dr. Brian Larry James. Dr. James shared his table with another scientist. What Mark didn't know is that the two of them were analyzing how well Mark was behaving in the dining-room and how well Rebel's "One-of-a-Kind Miracle Blood" was working to cure Mark's mind. They even paid Joseph to keep notes about what Mark was doing and saying.

At school, Mark's teachers regularly reported to the principal about how well he behaved in class and how well he treated his classmates. The principal passed the information on to the two scientists, without Mark knowing it.

Working with Mark was an eighteen-year-old full-time dishwasher name Lynnora, who suffered from bipolar disorder. She wanted to work her way up to the top position and become a restaurant owner, but she was told that it would be unrealistic due to her medical disability. She was very disappointed.

It was 10 A.M., the beginning of Lynnora's eight-hour shift. Joseph announced that the restaurant owner had cancelled free meals for all employees. Lynnora started to panic and freak out. She started begging her boss for a promotion so that she would have enough income to buy meals.

"Do you think that you can be independent handling food prep?" asked Joseph.

"I can give it a try, Joseph!" said Lynnora, talking a mile a minute.

"I don't think you have the ability to do food prep, Lynnora," said Joseph. "Your employment ability is limited."

"How about waitressing?" asked Lynnora getting even more excited. "Mark can always train me!"

Mark overheard his name being mentioned. He stood there listening to the whole conversation.

"Can you memorize which order belongs to which customer and which table?" asked Joseph.

"I can always practice!" said Lynnora, in a high-pitched voice.

"I am afraid you just don't have the skills," said Joseph. "I can tell by how you work. And by the way, don't you have a roommate to pitch in with the rent?"

"Uh…someone," said Lynnora, sounding caught for never mentioning it before.

"Is it a homeless person?" asked Joseph, beginning to be suspicious.

"Well, he's personally known to me," said Lynnora, sounding very nervous. He's my new boyfriend," said Lynnora. A bead of sweat dripped into her eye.

"So, if he's your new boyfriend, does he have a full-time job?" asked Joseph, with his arms crossed. He had a feeling that she was covering up something.

Lynnora's head started shaking. "Well, no but he's looking for work. He's willing to do anything to keep a roof over his head."

"Uh hmm," said Joseph, coming up with a plan to get the truth out of the scared girl, thinking she might be a victim of secret abuse at home. "You said that he'll do anything for work?"

"Yes."

"Tell him to come here and apply tomorrow morning," said Joseph, analyzing the girl's reaction. Then he asked her, "Why are you sweating and shaking your head?"

"I... I ...just... had a rough night," said Lynnora, without controlling her shakiness.

Joseph still had his arms crossed over his chest. Then he came up with an idea. "I'll tell you what. How about you take the rest of the day off and come back tomorrow morning with your boyfriend. I'll have Mark cover for you and you can go home now."

Lynnora felt relieved. She changed back into her street clothes and left for home.

Back in his office, Joseph was about to call Lynnora's doctor but it rang before he could pick up the handset. He answered it right away. "Kitchen department, Joseph speaking. Yes! You're the doctor of one of my employees? She was here this morning, but she was acting a bit suspicious, so I sent her home for the rest of the day ... Is she...? OK, I'll still be her reference even though she's on medical leave starting right away.

"Yes, she is a hard worker, very independent, fast, and well-organized. Also, she's reliable and punctual. She's very friendly and polite and well-mannered. She's one of my co-op employees. She has earned employee of the month. But I have quite a few concerns about her. She hardly socializes with her coworkers and she always sits alone from the crew.

"I overheard people say that she doesn't follow along with their conversations and doesn't comprehend their messages they tried to convey. Everybody's suggesting that she needs professional help. There's something suspicious about her. She said that she has a new boyfriend living with her and I was asking her if her boyfriend has a full-time job to pitch in with the rent.

"She never mentioned it to you? Oh, ha, she has been keeping secrets from the both of us the whole time. Now everything is making sense!

"OK, well, there's nothing for her to worry about. Again, I'm more than happy to give her a good reference.

"You, too. Bye-bye"

Chapter Four

The white wolf trotted down the highway in the valley between the mountains and into the forest where he stopped at a river. He swam across the river and climbed up the steep mountain slope, where rocks were falling past him.

He made his way to the top of a rock high up on the mountain, where he had a beautiful view of the highway, the forest and the lake. He sat on the top of the mountain rock, looking at the blue sky, where there was a flying bird.

The bird sent him a message from the heavenly Creator.

The wolf acknowledged the message: "WOOF!"

Chapter Five

In Edmonton, Robert Ryder and his buddies from the police academy, Bill and Will were having "Coffee with a Cop", a weekly routine with the public at McDonald's. The three of them were showing photos on their cell phones: the good old days in school, graduation photos, and more recent days of their police careers.

Robert was wearing an orange jersey with blue "OILERS" written on it. Bill and Will were dressed in their police uniforms. Bill asked Robert, "Who's the high school grad in that photo?"

"That's my nephew, Michael," said Robert. "He just graduated from high school and he's been accepted to study as a probation officer, just like his dad, my brother, Dave."

"Your brother was a probation officer?" Bill asked. "You never mentioned it to us before. What does he do now?"

"He recently became an RCMP officer."

"Cool! So, there's RCMP in the family!" said Will. "Hey, aren't you going to drink your coffee? You haven't had a sip ever since we came here."

Robert picked up his coffee and had a sip. All of a sudden, he made a face. "It tastes gross. Like ketchup!"

"Oh, Robert, you never said it tasted like ketchup before," said Will. "Here, let me have a sip."

"No! No! No! No!" Robert was freaking out.

Will picked up the cup and took a sip and then another sip. "It doesn't taste like ketchup. It tastes like pure honey like you normally add to your coffee." He turned to his other partner. "Bill, you try it and see how it tastes."

Bill took a couple of sips. "It tastes like pure honey to me," said Bill.

Will asked Robert, "are there any changes in your medication that we're not aware of?"

"Actually, I've been switched to a new drug," said Robert with a nervous laugh. "I had my first injection a couple of weeks ago and since then I've been taking pills."

"What about that other drug that you were prescribed?" asked Will, getting suspicious. "Why aren't you taking it?"

"Well, the old drug is no longer available because the drug company wasn't making enough profit. Pretty much all the patients are turning to this new drug that I am on right now. My doctor said that this new drug gives a quality of life which is ten times better than the old one. Hopefully, nothing goes wrong," said Robert with a worried look on his pale face.

"Why didn't you mention it to us before?" Bill asked with a serious concerned.

Robert's hand started shaking, "I didn't think it was necessary."

"You're shaking!" said Will, with serious concern. You look like you have lost a lot of weight! And you haven't been eating breakfast for the past two weeks. No wonder you didn't drink your coffee until I encouraged you to. I don't think this new drug you're on is working."

"And he said that the coffee tasted like ketchup, but you and I tasted the coffee for ourselves and it tasted like pure honey," added Bill.

Robert was anxious to leave the table to avoid their personal investigation. He said to them, "I've got to go grocery shopping and buy food! Bye!" and walked out of the restaurant.

Will said to Bill, "Robert sounds secretive and paranoid."

And Bill said, "I can see that. That's not like him. I don't think the new drug he's on is the right drug for him."

"I agree."

"Let's keep an eye on his behaviour." said Bill. "Let's go!"

...

That night, as Robert was putting on his pajamas and lying down in his bed, he suddenly heard sounds that seemed to be coming from the walls. He thought he was hearing sirens like a firetruck or an ambulance or police car. He closed his eyes to go to sleep.

Suddenly he saw Sasquatch, a character from the "The Six Million Dollar Man" TV series, attacking him. He covered his face for protection, feeling terrified.

...

The next morning, as Robert was walking to the washroom, he saw from the corner of his left eye what he thought was a string being pulled. Suddenly a bomb exploded in his mind! It freaked him out.

Throughout the rest of the week, Robert continued hallucinating. He avoided all the people he admired. He was terrified of them all, as well as himself!

One morning, he went into the living room and looked at his favorite painting of a white blue-eyed wolf that reminded him of his beloved dog, Rebel. He started whispering to the picture frame, feeling paranoid that somebody in the building could hear him.

"Tomorrow morning, Rebel, I'm planning to hitchhike all the way to Lake Louise to see you, so I can have your protection. Will you promise me to be my guardian angel?"

Chapter Six

The next morning, Robert wandered off from his apartment, suffering from hallucinations and paranoia. He came to a nearby gas station, still wearing his "Oilers" jersey. He hopped on the back of a truck and hid underneath some blankets.

The truck owner came out of the store, after paying for gas, and climbed into the driver's seat. He buckled up, started the engine, and drove off, without being aware that there was somebody on the back of the vehicle. The truck had a customized Alberta license plate that said "LOUISE" with a picture sticker of a lake.

...

Robert woke up after a long drive, looked at his watch and realized it had been an eight-hour ride. He climbed down off the back of the truck at the next gas station, making sure he was not seen by the owner or anyone. He recognized the environment surrounded by mountains -- he was in Lake Louise.

Robert set out walking along the ditch by a quiet highway in the forest. At one point, a tree branch caught his shin and he left behind a few drops of blood.

He walked deeper into the forest, leaving footprints in the soft soil. Finally, he arrived at his favorite spot by the pond. He was tired after such a long walk and he lay down on the grass and fell asleep.

...

Two hours later, Robert woke up and was relieved to see the white blue-eyed wolf of his dreams standing there, looking harmless.

Robert said to the wolf, "Am I dreaming? Are you real? What are you doing standing there? Are you an angel or are you rebel?"

The wolf didn't respond. Instead, it, turned around as if to lead Robert to the pond.

Robert followed the silent wolf, stopped, and stood there looking into the pond, without knowing what was happening.

Behind him, the angel wolf spoke to him, "Just look at the reflection in the pond and you'll remember how irrational your behaviour was during your university days."

In the reflection of the pond ...

A university teacher confronted Robert, "I can't read your messy handwriting, Robert! From now on, I want to see your neatest handwriting, or next time, you'll be given zero! Is that understood?"

"Understood."

He could hear other students. One said, "That guy over there, he's always pairing with teachers! He never socializes with us as his own peers!"

Another student said, "I know! And I heard that he made a strange comment about the two teachers! And he thinks it's funny! I mean that comment doesn't make sense!"

Robert approached the students at the cafeteria, making an effort to get their attention. And it was not the first time. Those two students could see that he was begging for friendship, but instead, they just left.

At the library, an English student confronted Robert when he approached, saying , "I don't want to talk to you anymore! You betrayed me for the guy over there! I don't know what you see in him!" And then he left the library and never spoke to Robert again.

In the same place, a second English student got frustrated with Robert and said, "Robert, don't believe everything that guy says, he's a storyteller! And common sense would ask, 'What would he do with these mountains?' Do you really think he owns that much of a big property? THINK!"

And a third student got annoyed with Robert and said, "Can't you see that I'm busy with my English assignment? I don't have time for anybody! Don't take it personally!"

In English class, a teacher scolded Robert for his behaviour and his way of shaking hands. "No, Robert. You don't shake hands like you are a dead fish! That's not polite! You squeeze! No, you don't squeeze so hard! You use a firm grip! That's better! You see how gentle a firm grip feels?"

"You don't have to be told how to shake people's hands! You should think for yourself and use common sense! No wonder I hear people making comments about your unusual behaviour! I'm concerned about you, and so are all your teachers. I recommend that you see a psychiatrist."

… and then Robert returned to the present day …

The angel wolf behind him said, "Why don't you go back and lay down, Robert, it's going to be a very long, long night."

Robert turned around and asked the wolf if it was him that was speaking, but the white wolf would not answer. Instead, the wolf turned around and led Robert to his sleeping spot. Robert lay down on the ground and instantly fell into a deep sleep, with the angel white wolf guarding him.

Robert began dreaming about a hockey game with players in dark shadows…

Chapter Seven

At the gym where Mark worked out on his days off, the gym owner, Steve Maxwell, analyzed Mark's behaviour and how he related to other gym members. He wrote everything down for the scientist and psychiatrist who paid him. They needed the information for their experiment.

A couple of twenty-something members, Samuel and Ben, were talking in the corner. "Mark is such an awesome guy," said Samuel. "He would spot me on chest presses by supporting me to keep pushing every rep possible. And you know what?"

"What?"

"He would say. 'Push it! Push it the hard way!' I broke my record because of him!"

"He would do the same thing to me when he was spotting me on bicep curls!" said the Ben. "He wouldn't give up on me until I was completely destroyed!"

"Ha!"

"He really boosted my confidence! He's really mature for an 18-year-old!"

"Yes, he is, just by the way he behaves. I really enjoy having him around!" replied Samuel.

A third friend, Calvin, joined the conversation. "That Mark guy over there … he trains the night away. No wonder he developed so quickly and has the best results. Also, he is very patient."

"He also keeps to himself," said Jason, joining the group. "He respects everyone's boundaries and hardly says a word, but he's very friendly and sociable when he's off the training floor. I really admire him."

Steve had also noted that Mark trained the right way. He paid close attention to the positive comments from the two gym members.

Mark finished his training for the evening, changed into his street clothes and went outside to untie his waiting dog, Buddy. Then they walked home together.

Chapter Eight

Rihanna arrived at Shaunabell's cottage. So far, she was having a normal day.

"Is that yours?" asked Rihanna, pointing to the black German Shepherd.

"Yes, he is now," answered Shaunabell. "My son discovered the dog on a floating wooden raft that came from out of nowhere. He asked me if we could keep him and I told him we were glad to."

"What's the dog's name?"

"Buddy."

"Buddy? Well, that's a cool name for a dog," said Rihanna.

"Oh, by the way, Buddy needs his fur shaved," said Shaunabell. "That's why I called you."

"OK. Here, I'll start by giving him a good shave with the dog razor. Buddy, come over here."

Even though he had never met this stranger before, Buddy obeyed and stood there, ready for his whole body to be shaved.

"Good boy, Buddy!" said Rihanna. "Now, stay still, I'm giving you a real good shave... How do you like your new fur coat?"

"WOOF!"

"You do like it don't you, you, Buddy?" said Rihanna with a cheerful smile.

"WOOF!"

"You know," Rihanna said to Shaunabell. "Dogs really enjoy the beauty of nature."

"Yes, they do," said Shaunabell. "Dogs can really see how beautiful nature is. It's part of their animal nature."

Rihanna interrupted. "Anyways, I am also here to share my personal announcement with you."

"Oh? Well, let's sit down and you can tell me what you want to share with me. I'm listening."

The two friends took seats at the picnic table.

"Today's my last day for shaving dogs for you," Rihanna began. "My house is up for sale. So far, I haven't heard from anyone who is interested in buying my property. I spent a lot of time renovating it all by myself. I hope it looks inviting and welcoming. I'm crossing my fingers that somebody out there will offer me a good deal for it, since it's in good condition."

"I'm quite confident that you'll get a decent offer pretty soon," said Shaunabell.

"WOOF!"

"Even Buddy has the faith that someone out there will give you an offer you can't turn down."

"I just have to pray and set my hopes up."

"That's all you have to do, Rihanna is pray. By the way, would like to have a cup of iced tea? It's pretty hot out here."

"No, thank you," said Rihanna not wanting to take her friend for granted.

"It's OK, Rihanna. I insist that you accept for the first time ever since I've known you. It makes me feel good that I share my refreshments with others. Here, let me pour you a cup. It's really fresh!"

"OK, I accept," said Rihanna feeling a little guilty, since she was unaccustomed to accepting offers.

Chapter Nine

At Mental Health Services, Mark had just finished his session with the therapist. "You can go now, Mark," said the therapist. "I'll walk you to the waiting room."

They walked in silence to the waiting room. Mark was surprised to see his parents sitting there. "Mom, dad? What are you two doing here?"

They ignored his question. The therapist approached them in greeting. "Hello there, Mr. and Mrs. Barker. Come this way to my office. Mark, please sit down."

Mark didn't expect this, and was confused. He could not understand why it was kept as a secret. He sat down and wondered, "What's this all about?"

As the therapist walked back to his office with Mark's parents he said, "I'm, Nicolas. I want you to meet two important people who are waiting in my office."

They entered the office to see two men sitting there. The therapist introduced Mark's parents. "This is Simon Barker and his wife Shaunabell."

Turning back, he said, "Simon and Shaunabell, this is Dr. Brian Larry James, a psychiatrist, and this is Dr. Pierre Royal Mackenzie, a scientist doing top-secret research."

All four exchanged "Hi's" and handshakes.

"Have a seat, everyone, and make yourselves comfortable." He turned to the scientist. "You may begin, Dr. MacKenzie"

The scientist began, "We have incredible news. Dr. James and I have an announcement to make about the results for your son, Mark.

"You two always knew that I had you raise Mark as your own son. His life has been a miracle ever since he received a transfusion of a blood substance from Rebel, the deceased half-wolf and half-German Shepherd. Rebel was the one and only in this world with the blessed substance that we named 'Rebel's One-of-a-Kind Miracle Blood'. This substance has been keeping your boy in reality ever since he was diagnosed with bipolar disorder and schizophrenia at five years of age, disorders that he inherited from his biological parents.

"According to information from Robert Ryder, Rebel's owner, Rebel died saving Mark when he was five. Mark had been left stranded on a yellow rubber boat on the lake. Rebel was a hero, risking his own life to save Mark, even though he had no swimming experience.

"'Rebel's One-of-a-Kind Miracle Blood' contains a substance that improves quality of life for bipolar disorder and schizophrenia patients. Your son's mission is to provide transfusions of this substance to as many patients as he can, for the rest of his life. He will become a hospital resident and that will be his permanent home in Edmonton.

"As it turns out," continued the scientist. "I am familiar with Robert Ryder and he also suffers from schizophrenia. He will be the first one to be treated with this substance. If it works for him, we will then move on to providing transfusions to other patients.

"Unfortunately, Robert has gone missing. Your son's time has come. His first task is to find Robert before it's too late! The drug Robert is on is not strong enough, so he's going to get very sick!"

Their meeting was almost over, but the scientist had one more alarming announcement for Simon and Shaunabell. "Oh, by the way. The whole world is in danger without your son! There are dangerous German criminals looking everywhere for Mark.

"They are on trial in California. One of the two witnesses against these criminals needs to be convinced to receive a transfusion of 'Rebel's One-of-a-Kind Miracle Blood' before the court will allow her to testify against the criminals. The Canadian and United States governments are counting on the both of you to keep Mark safe and alive! Good luck!"

Chapter Ten

On her second visit to Shaunabell's cottage, Rihanna got out of her car and started jumping up and down, singing and dancing non-stop, high as a kite.

Shaunabell was sitting on her beach chair, wearing sunglasses and a hat, waiting for Buddy to come out of the water after doing many laps as part of his swimming lessons. As the dog returned, Shaunabell was startled by the super high-pitched screaming and singing. She turned around and saw it was Rihanna running towards her, like a happy young child with her arms wide open, looking super-excited as if she had super-good news to announce.

"Shaunabell! Shaunabell! I'm so happy! I'm so happy! I'm on top of the world! I'm on top of the world!"

"Calm down, Rihanna!" said Shaunabell. "Calm down! Tell me what you came to tell me!"

Rihanna continued jumping up and down singing and dancing. "I'm so happy! I'm so happy! I'm on top of the world. I'm on top of the world!"

"Calm down Rihanna! Calm down!"

Rihanna continued singing and dancing until suddenly Buddy stepped in to support Shaunabell. "WOOF!"

Rihanna stopped abruptly at the sound of the bark.

"Now, Rihanna, take a deep breath," said Shaunabell. "That's right! There you go! Do you feel better? Have a seat and tell me what you have to tell me."

Rihanna took a deep breath and sat down. Then she started talking rapidly. "I just had an email from the real estate agent about a lady in Edmonton. She offered to buy my house for DOUBLE the asking price. Also, she offered me a beautiful salon at the local hospital in Edmonton at no charge."

"Well, that's very generous of that lady. It sounds like she was desperate to be the first one to purchase your property and get it over with, before someone else could buy it. That lady must've appreciated how well the property was crafted. You should feel blessed for that kind of generosity. I would be. It's only once in a lifetime.

"Anyways, would you like to have a hotdog and a cup of iced tea? Or are you going to say 'no thank you' again this time?"

"I am really thirsty," said Rihanna, smiling and feeling confident. "But I won't have time because I've got to get home and do the rest of my packing before my movers show up tomorrow morning. Then I have to get to bed early. Do you have a spare container to put some iced tea in, so I can take it with me?"

"Great idea!" said Shaunabell, agreeing with her. "Wait here. I'll be right back."

Shaunabell left the picnic table and returned right away. "Here's a container of iced tea and here's a box of Kool-Aid powder. They are yours to use on your long trip to Edmonton. It's my gift to you for your wonderful friendship."

"Thank you," said Rihanna. "I really appreciate it." Then she let out a big sigh.

"You look pretty worn out after all that excitement. How about if Buddy and I walk you to your car? How does that sound?"

"Sounds great to me!" said Rihanna with confidence.

"Let's walk," said Shaunabell. Then she said to the dog, "Come with me, Buddy. We're walking Rihanna to her car."

They walked out to the car and said their goodbyes. Shaunabell watched her friend drive away, heading for home. That was farewell for Rihanna.

Chapter Eleven

Three days later, Shaunabell was sitting at the picnic table again, reading the provincial newspaper, while Buddy was doing laps in the water. There was an announcement in the newspaper about Rebel's thirteenth year death anniversary. While Shaunabell was reading, she heard a car pull into her driveway. Unexpectedly, it was Rihanna.

Shaunabell thought; "What's Rihanna doing here? I thought she had already left for Edmonton this morning. What does she want this time? She looks so depressed all of a sudden. That's not like her. I wonder what's on her mind."

Rihanna was walking slowly towards the picnic table with her head down like she was walking dead. Shaunabell invited her to sit down. Rihanna plopped on the chair, with the provincial newspaper in her hand.

"Hi, Rihanna. I wasn't expecting you to be here at this hour. It's quite early. I thought you had already left for Edmonton. You look so depressed, it's not like you. Are you looking forward to start a new fresh life in Edmonton? What's on your mind?"

"This morning," said Rihanna feeling emotional with tears. "I was reading the provincial newspaper article about the remembrance of Rebel's 13th year death anniversary. I was the animal breeder of his parents. That's how he was born, remember?"

"Yes, Rihanna, I remember," said Shaunabell, offering her a Kleenex. "I was also reading about the heroic dog this morning."

Buddy was lying down, listening to the conversation.

"He was a brave dog when he saved that stranded five-year-old boy's life, even though he had no swimming experience," said Rihanna wiping her eyes with Kleenex. "That's how Mark came to be given to you and Simon for legal adoption."

"Without you and Rebel," said Shaunabell, as she put her hand on Rihanna's, "my son wouldn't be here to make a difference for others."

Rihanna was confused. "What do I have to do with this? Why did God pick Mark and me to go on living? Is there something that I don't know?"

"Yes, but everything is strictly confidential," replied Shaunabell.

"OK, but you still haven't answered my question. What do you have to do with it?" Then Rihanna started sobbing. "What have I done? It sounds like there's no purpose for me in this life!"

Rihanna continued sobbing. Shaunabell was becoming more concerned. Buddy got up from the ground and put his chin on Rihanna's lap.

"Even Buddy is telling you that there is always a rainbow after a bad storm. He's giving you angel advice."

"Angel advice, huh?" Said Rihanna. "It sounds like Buddy is telling me that there's a future with… with professional counseling. I am right?"

"WOOF!"

Shaunabell smiled, indicating that it was a good idea. Rihanna returned the smile with confidence. They exchanged hugs and goodbyes, then Rihanna left the picnic table and off she went to Edmonton for a fresh beginning.

"WOOF!"

Chapter Twelve

In the backyard of the restaurant, where Buddy was waiting for Mark to get off work, he caught the scent of two important people and took off to track them down. He ran across the road to the park and there he found a man and a woman sleeping in ragged sleeping bags. He silently approached them and lay down between them, licking the man's face.

The homeless man woke up, startled, and said, "Get lost! You woke me up!"

The dog turned to face the homeless woman. She put her arm on Buddy's forehead and kissed the dog on the nose. Suddenly she woke up and realized it was not her husband she was kissing. She saw the black German Shepherd looking at her and started freaking out. "Ugh! Shoo! Go away!"

The dog just lay there, refusing to budge. The homeless couple got up and started to walk away. They ordered the dog, "Stay there!" The dog obeyed and stayed where he was, without moving a muscle.

The couple were several feet away from the dog when they overheard a conversation between a mother and son that was just loud enough for her to make out what the mother was saying.

"Honey, you're five years old today. It's time that I start teaching you to respect animals. You shouldn't ignore an animal when it is trying to get your attention. It could be very important. For example, you see that the black German Shepherd over there lying on the ground?"

"Yah?" said the little boy.

"Well, that black German Shepherd could be an angel sent by the Heavenly Creator..."

The conversation sounded familiar to the homeless woman, and it brought back memories.

She turned to her husband. "That conversation I just overheard sounds familiar. This is exactly the same spot where we were teaching our son to respect animals. That was thirteen years ago, when he was just five years old. Do you remember?"

"Yes, of course!" said her husband. Suddenly, he was hoping for a miracle.

"That black German Shepherd back there approached us for a reason," said the woman. "Let's go back there and check it out and see what he's trying to tell us."

"I agree. Let's go."

They walked back to the dog. Buddy rolled over on his back.

"He wants us to rub his belly!" said the woman, with a laugh. They both leaned over and rubbed the dog's belly. Then, the dog sat up and held out his right paw.

"Oh, a paw shake?" said the man. And they both laughed and shook the dog's paw with enjoyment.

"I'm a bit hungry and thirsty," said the homeless wife.

"Me too."

Buddy quickly responded with a bark, "WOOF!" Then he led them across the street, to the backyard of the restaurant, and waited for his master to come out.

Seconds later, Mark stepped out of the back door with a large plastic bag for the garbage bin. He stopped, looked at them, and asked in a polite manner, "Hi, there. May I help you both?"

"Does this dog belong to you?" asked the homeless man.

"No, not really," answered Mark. "I discovered him on a floating raft on the lake at my cottage. Why, are you guys familiar with the dog? Is it yours by any chance?"

"No," said the homeless man. "My wife and I were sleeping at the park and the dog woke me up by licking my face."

"And me, too. I thought I was kissing my husband but when I woke up, I discovered I was kissing the dog's nose. It really freaked me out!" said the woman.

"So, the sleeping bags in your hands tell me that both of you live on the streets without a roof over your head?" asked Mark, with concern.

"Yes, and it's a long story," said the homeless couple.

"I suppose you guys are hungry and thirsty. I'll tell you what. You two can have a seat on these boxes. I'll bring each of you some hotdogs with ketchup, mustard, and relish, and a glass of iced tea. My boss won't mind. Wait here, I'll be right back."

Mark went back into the kitchen and came back with two plates of hotdogs, some chocolate chip cookies and two glasses of iced tea. Mark sat down with the hungry couple. "So, tell me your story, if you guys don't mind," said Mark, with interest.

The man spoke first. "I once had a job as a high-paid waiter and then became the dining room manager. But I started to suffer from schizophrenia. Now I'm unable to hold a job."

Then the woman told her story. "I was 12 when I graduated from high school. For three years, I earned money by babysitting and that paid my university fees. I earned my university degree in medicine in four years, instead of seven years.

"But, by the time I started my own practice in psychiatry, I started to get sick. Now I suffer from bipolar disorder and I can't function in any type of work."

"I'm sorry to hear what the both of you went through," said Mark. "I'm also a top-paid waiter. And I was too smart for school. My dad allowed me to jump three grades, no more than that. I graduated when I was 15. I'm already expected to study medicine in university."

Then Mark noticed that the two homeless people were deep in thoughts. "The two of you look like you're sad. Is something on your mind?"

"Well, eighteen years ago, my wife and I …" the homeless man began, with tears.

"…had a son together." The homeless woman finished the sentence. "We ended up on welfare."

"Our son was taken away from us when he was five," said the emotional homeless man. "Then we lost our welfare payments and ended up on the streets."

"How about we all hold hands together and say a prayer?" said Mark. Then he reached for their hands and held them.

"Dear God, the Heavenly Father," Mark began praying. "Please help these two people get medical care so they can live normal lives. And better government housing. But most of all, please bring their son back into their lives, so they can be reunited as a family. Please do all of these things as a blessing to them. Thank you, God, the Heavenly Father, for listening to our prayer. Amen."

"Amen."

The black German Shepherd looked up at the sparkling stars in the night sky and saw them as a sign of promise. The homeless couple got up and went back to the park.

Mark headed home with his pet dog, Buddy.

Chapter Thirteen

Mark and Buddy walked through the door, and he said, "Hi, mom! Hi, dad! Sorry, that I'm late for supper. I'll get ready for dinner and join you."

Mark took off his shoes and went to the washroom where he washed his hands with liquid soap and dried his hands with a towel. He went back to the dining room and joined his parents at the table, where supper was already set out. There was spaghetti and shepherd's pie and green salad. Buddy was already eating his dinner from his bowl, on the floor next to Simon.

"Mom? Dad?", said Mark.

"Yes, son?"

"I have something very important to bring up."

"Go ahead, we're listening," said Simon.

"I found a homeless couple in the backyard at my workplace, when I was about to take out the garbage at the end of my shift. The homeless man asked me about Buddy. He wanted to know if he belonged to me. I said no and told him how I discovered Buddy. Then he told me how he and his wife were approached by the dog at the park.

"I don't know what made Buddy go there and approach them. Maybe Buddy had a reason. I don't know what he was thinking. Maybe Buddy brought them over because they were hungry. So, I offered them some hotdogs and iced tea and chocolate cookies.

"After they finished eating, they told me about how they ended up on the streets. They said they both suffered from mental disorders that prevent them from functioning on the job.

"One had a full-time job as a dining room manager. The other one graduated high school at age 12 and has her university degree in medicine. She really sounds like she's gifted. That is something I have in common with these two homeless people.

"Oh! One sad thing they mentioned was how they had a son that was taken away from them thirteen years ago when he was five. Their son must be eighteen now, same age as me. So, I held their hands and said a prayer that their son will be reunited with them.

"Anyway, mom and dad. I'm grateful that you two gave me the first breath when I was born and that I was never taken away from you like their son was. You two still love me because I'm..."

Simon and Shaunabell looked at each other, thinking it might be the right time to reveal the secret about Mark's past.

"Mom? Dad?" asked Mark, with a surprised look. "Is something wrong?"

Shaunabell said to her husband, "Our son needs to know the truth about his past. Can I tell him?"

Simon answered his wife with confidence. "No, I'll tell him myself." He turned his attention back to Mark and began telling the true story. The black German Shepherd lay there, listening.

"There is a story that you need to know, Mark. And it's the right time for you to hear this.

"Thirteen years ago, there was a five-year-old boy who was stranded on a yellow rubber boat in the middle of the lake. The little boy was rescued by a half-wolf and half German Shepherd even though he had no swimming experience.

"Days later, the dog died due to over-exertion from swimming. A scientist working on a top-secret project drained all the blood from the dead animal and studied the blood in a research lab. He discovered that the blood contained a substance that improves quality of life for individuals with bipolar disorder and schizophrenia. Then he learned that the five-year-old boy had been taken away from his parents who suffered from these mental disorders.

"This young boy was also diagnosed with both bipolar disorder and schizophrenia. The scientist chose the young child as a test subject and he was transfused with the animal blood.

"To collect data on how well the treatment has been working for the boy, the scientist has been working in secret with his school teachers, a gym owner and the boy's employer. They all keep notes on how well his brain is behaving.

"The scientist named the cure 'Rebel's one-of-a-kind Miracle Blood' after the half-wolf and half German Shepherd.

"The boy is now an adult at age eighteen, and his time has come to start his lifelong mission of transfusing the miracle blood to all individuals with bipolar disorder and schizophrenia!"

Slowly, Mark realized that the story that his dad was telling him was all about him, the whole time. "So, you're telling me that I'm adopted?"

Both parents nodded their heads. Mark was shocked, feeling emotionally hurt. A tear dripped from his left eye.

Then he said, "So, the homeless couple that I just fed supper must be my birth parents. Everything is making sense to me. I have a lot in common with them in my genes. For example, the homeless woman graduated when she was twelve and now has a university degree in medicine. I inherited her gift and brain."

Suddenly, Mark flipped out on the parents who had raised him. "DO YOU TWO REALIZE WHAT MY REAL PARENTS HAVE BEEN GOING

THROUGH SINCE THEIR SON WAS STOLEN FROM THEM? AND I HAVE BEEN TREATED LIKE A SECRET PROJECT THE WHOLE TIME!"

"Son, settle down," said Simon, in a firm voice.

Mark began hollering, "WHY SHOULD I?"

Shaunabell stepped in to support Simon. "Mark, hollering in this house is unacceptable! I will not put up with it! Now, let your father tell you what is happening. It's very important, and you need to know!"

"Now, son, take a deep breath," said Simon with gentle courage.

Mark did as he was told.

"That's right," said Simon. "That's a good boy."

Mark became quiet, but he was still upset. Simon began talking. "You have been chosen by the Heavenly Father and so has Rebel. The whole world is in a …"

"I don't want to hear any more of this!" Mark stood up quickly and ran to his room.

"Mark, come back here!" demanded Simon. "It's rude to walk away from the table when I'm still talking to you!"

"Let him be, Simon," said Shaunabell, firmly. "He's not ready to listen to everything you have to tell him. Let Mother Nature decide when the time is right."

Mark put on his pajamas and went to bed. Before he turned off his lamp, he looked at the childhood photograph of himself sitting on his dad's lap, beside his mom. In anger, he turned the photograph towards the wall and switched off his lamp.

Chapter Fourteen

It was eleven o'clock at night. Simon and Shaunabell were in bed, sleeping. Mark sneaked out of the cottage, making sure he did not wake up his parents. He passed by Buddy, where he was sleeping outside next to the front door. Mark walked quickly down to the end of the dock, untied the motorboat and climbed in. Instead of starting the motor, he started paddling, so that no one would hear him leave.

"Now, I have privacy," Mark thought to himself.

"Hmm. Out here in the middle of the lake looks familiar. I'm beginning to remember…

"I was stranded all alone on a yellow rubber boat when I was five … thirteen years ago. And a half-wolf half-German Shepherd heard my cry and jumped into the water to rescue me.

"But the dog started to struggle in the water and both the dog and I had to be rescued by his master, a teenager who called himself 'Wolf' but his real name was Robert. And I remember that the dog was called… Rebel!

"And Wolf's girlfriend took the three of us for a boat ride and Wolf was making me laugh by telling me jokes.

"But then I was handed over to two police officers, a man and a woman. Then I was handed over to a scientist —the one who transfused blood from that dog who saved my life.

"Then I was turned over to the Barkers for legal adoption. And my natural parents? ... I believe I just met them at the backyard when I was about to take out the garbage shortly before my shift was over...

"It was Buddy that found them after all this time! Their story sounds familiar! Oh, thank you, God, the Heavenly Father, you answered my prayer! I must go back home, to my two moms and dads!"

All of a sudden, there was a flash of lightning and it started 'raining cats and dogs.' Mark started freaking out, because he was terrified of storms. He tried to start the engine, but it wouldn't catch.

He started padding the boat, but it was filling up with water and quickly sank below the water. Mark feared for his safety, and he desperately looked around for his life jacket. It was nowhere to be found! He had forgotten it! Mark realized that he had to swim back to shore on his own!

. . .

As the young troubled boy was struggling to keep his head above the water he cried out for help: "MOM! DADDY! HELP ME! SOMEBODY SAVE ME!"

Back at the cottage, Buddy woke up when he heard the cry. He immediately ran to the end of the dock, jumped into the water, and began paddling as fast as he could towards the troubled boy.

Mark was still struggling, barely keeping his head above water.

Buddy kept paddling confidently, as fast as he could.

Mark was getting scared and tired.

Buddy was still not giving up. He started paddling even faster.

Mark was almost exhausted, but kept trying to keep his head above water.

Buddy was getting closer and closer to the tiring boy.

Mark was starting to lose his strength.

Buddy could sense the struggling boy's weak breathing, he barked twice to encourage him to keep hanging in there.

"WOOF! WOOF!"

Mark heard the barking and was relieved that his rescuer had arrived. It gave him a boost.

When the dog touched the struggling boy, Mark put his arms around his rescuer's neck for support. The dog turned around and headed back to the shore with the boy.

Back at the cottage, Simon and Shaunabell were still sleeping. A loud clap of thunder woke them up. Shaunabell noticed that she did not hear Mark freaking out, as he normally would. That was not like him, she thought, so she went to his room to check on him.

When she turned on his lamp, she saw that he was not in bed. Then she noticed that the family photograph was turned facing the wall. Right away, she realized that her son must have run away.

Shaunabell rushed back to her bedroom and woke Simon, telling him that Mark was missing. Simon jumped out of bed and dialed 911.

. . .

Mark and Buddy were halfway back to the dock, when Simon, now in his paramedic uniform, arrived in an ambulance boat with his coworkers. Simon climbed down the ladder and pulled his troubled son to safety.

The other paramedics lifted the rescue dog up onto the boat. Buddy shook off all the water. They petted him said, "Good boy, Buddy! You did an awesome job!"

. . .

Simon was relieved that his boy was safe, but he was not in a good mood to talk to his child. He was angry because of the way Mark had reacted at suppertime.

Mark sat on a chair with a towel wrapped around him, while the paramedics checked his blood pressure. He started apologizing to his father, "I'm sorry, Dad, for how I—"

"Don't call me 'Dad!'" Simon purposely snapped loud enough for his paramedic colleagues to hear, knowing that they would understand. "And don't even look at me!"

The ambulance boat returned to the dock. There were two police officers waiting for them. Shaunabell was standing there, too, with the police, with relief that her boy was safe. But she was also very upset with how Mark had acted, without thinking about the consequences.

Simon stepped onto the dock with a tight grip on Mark's arm. Mark started apologizing to his mother, "Mom, I'm sorry how I—"

"Don't call me, 'Mom', young man!" Shaunabell snapped. And don't even look at me! You can look at those two police officers who are going to take you into custody!"

The two police officers nodded, to show that they understood what Shaunabell and Simon had in mind.

Mark started panicking, begging the police not to arrest him. "No, please don't arrest me! It wasn't like you thought! It never crossed my mind!"

But the police handcuffed Mark, saying, "You are under arrest for your careless actions. You have the right to remain silent."

The officers took Mark to a prison and led him to a cell that was already occupied by two inmates.

"Here are prisoners that we want you to meet before you become one of them," said one of the officers. Then he turned to the inmates. "You and you! Start talking! Tell this guy what's happening!"

One of the inmates started talking. "I'm a dangerous German criminal! The whole world is in danger of being kidnapped by our secret criminal spies!"

The second one joined in, "Once the cops open this cell of ours we'll take care of you!"

"Ha! Ha! Ha!" Both inmates laughed in an evil-sounding way.

Mark was scared of what was going to happen. He turned to the police officers. "Officers, I realize how important I am to the both of you, my family, and the global community. I'm willing to hear the rest of the story from my folks who raised me. I'm sorry that I scared you and got you all upset. Will you please forgive me?"

"Of course," said one of the officers. "Now we're in business."

"We'll drive you back home," said the other officer. "The authorities have been protecting you ever since day one. Let's go!"

...

Back at the cottage, Simon and Shaunabell were having a private conversation in the living room. They heard a knock on their door. When Shaunabell answered the door, she met the same two officers returning Mark.

"Oh, hi, come on in," said Shaunabell, as she greeted them at the door." Come and join us in the dining room. Do you want a glass of water?"

"No, that's okay, but thanks anyway," said the two officers. "We're here to return your miracle son. Can we all have a chat for a couple of minutes in front of your son?"

"Of course," said Simon. "Have a seat and make yourselves comfortable."

All five of them seated themselves at the dining room table, with Mark sitting between the two police officers, and the two parents opposite them.

One of the policemen said to Mark, "Mark, can you tell your folks what you have learned from our conversation on the way here?

"Sure, of course. I'll be glad to tell my ... ummm..."

"You can call us Mom and Dad," said Simon. "Family doesn't always require blood. Family requires…"

"LOVE!" Mark finished the sentence for his dad.

"That's my boy!" said the proud father." Go on and tell us what you have to say."

Mark told them what he had learned. "At the prison, I met two inmates. They said to me that they're dangerous German criminals who would take care of me once these two police officers left me in their hands. I got so scared! I realized how important I am to the police and the global community.

"I was told that there are two valuable witnesses who are needed to testify against these criminals. One of the witnesses may behave oddly but she's full of rich knowledge in those criminals' histories. She was a criminal psychiatrist before she got sick with schizophrenia. The court won't allow her in the courtroom until she returns to one hundred percent reality and she needs Rebel's One-of-a-kind Miracle Blood to get there. I'm the only one who can provide a transfusion of this.

"I really don't want to see all of us become slaves of the Germans. This is how important I am to everybody."

"Well, I'm glad that you know the full truth," said Simon. Then he said to the two police officers, "Anything else we need to talk about?"

"That's all," said the policeman. "Our conversation is over. We've got to get going."

They got up from the table and walked to the door with Simon and Shaunabell.

"Thank you, officers," they said. "We appreciate your service and protection."

"Wait! Before you go…" said Mark to the two officers. "Thank you for teaching me a valuable lesson, especially about what those two dangerous inmates would do to me if you placed me behind bars with them. Like I said, you, your families, and our global community come first."

"BINGO!" said the policeman. "Make sure that you focus on your own risk. We're all counting on you, buddy!"

The police woman winked at Mark with a smile, as the went out the door. It was four-thirty in the morning when the whole family finally went back to bed.

Chapter Fifteen

Back in the woods, Robert was still in a deep sleep, dreaming about the hockey rink. He saw players in black shadows and royal blue, surrounding the white skating ice rink. The players passed the puck to one another and the crowd was roaring. The spectators were all around the rink and he was sitting in the upper seats, way up near the ceiling.

The dream kept speeding on and on. Robert kept shaking his head from side to side, like the dream was driving him crazy!

The white blue-eyed angel wolf just stood there guarding the deep sleeping young man.

Chapter Sixteen

It was eight o'clock in the morning in Edmonton and two police officers, Bill and Will, were sitting in McDonald's after a session with the public that they called "Coffee with a Cop."

Their friend, Robert, wasn't there, and the two officers were suspicious that something must be wrong with him.

They noticed a young fellow sitting at a table by himself. He looked familiar, and after a moment, they remembered who he was. They approached the familiar-looking guy.

"Excuse me, you must be Michael, the nephew of Robert Ryder. Am I correct?" said Will, with a friendly smile.

"Yes, I am," answered Michael, returning the smile. "Please have a seat and join me."

Will and Bill seated themselves.

"I suppose that my Uncle Robert knows the both of you personally?" said Michael. "Am I correct?"

"Yes, you are, my friend," answered Will. "I'm Will and this is my partner and friend, Bill."

"Hi, Michael. How are you?" said Bill. They exchanged handshakes.

"So," said Michael, "you guys and Uncle Robert went to police academy together?"

"That's right, Michael," they replied.

"Anyway, Bill and I have a very important conversation that we want to start with you," said Will. "Your Uncle Robert and Bill and I normally have coffee together as a regular weekly routine. He's missed two meetings in a row and that's not like him. Have you noticed anything unusual about your uncle, lately?"

"Actually, Uncle Robert didn't respond to our text messages when my parents and I were on a three-week vacation in Hawaii. We thought that was strange... I mean, that's not like him to stay so silent. He normally responds right away.

"My dad is an RCMP officer and he has had experience with that type of silence. And my mom is a pharmacist and she is also familiar with that type of odd behaviour – especially from patients who were mistakenly switched to the wrong treatment for schizophrenia. They started suffering from hallucinations and paranoia, and ended up in the hospital.

We know the name of the drug Uncle Robert was switched to, and we have a gut feeling that Uncle Robert might end up getting lost, you know, wandering away from the city."

Suddenly the nephew made the connection. "Oh, no. Uncle Robert is lost! He must've wandered away! Let's go to his apartment and see if we can figure out where he went."

"OK, Michael, take us to your uncle's place!" ordered Bill. "Where does he live?"

Michael pointed through the window across the parking lot. "Over there on the other side of the road!"

"Let's go!" said Will.

...

The three of them arrived at Robert's apartment building and called the caretaker to let them into the apartment. Bill and Will went carefully through the rooms.

In the kitchen, they discovered that the fridge was empty and in need of cleaning.

In the bedroom, they discovered that the bed was unmade and Robert's iPhone was still plugged in. There was an empty prescription bottle on the side table, along with a painting of a white blue-eyed wolf against a background of mountains, forests and a sunlit lake. The painting had a title: "Lake Louise." The officers could see a place on the wall where the painting would normally hang.

"Uhh, Michael?" asked Will, reading the title on the photo painting. "Where did your Uncle Robert buy this painting?"

"In Lake Louise. Why?" Michael answered.

Will didn't respond. Instead, he asked Bill to look at the painting. After a moment, they realized that Robert must have gone to Lake Louise. But they needed more evidence to prove that Robert really went there.

"Michael, let's go to the police station," said Will.

As they were leaving the apartment, they noticed a woman unloading shopping bags from her car. "That's my uncle's neighbour. Maybe she can be a help," said Robert."

The two police officers approached the woman. "Excuse me, ma'am?" said Will." Is Robert your neighbour?"

"Yes, he is. Why?"

"Have you noticed anything unusual about him lately?"

"Actually, I've noticed that there hasn't been any of the usual sounds coming from his apartment, like the television or the cellphone ringing. It's been about three weeks," the neighbour stated.

"The last time I saw him, he knocked on my door around nine at night, right when I was about to go to bed. He asked me to come to his apartment and see if I could hear any odd sounds.

"I went in there and listened for about five minutes. I told him honestly that I didn't hear anything. He told me that he could hear a loud spinning wheel sound, like a washing machine or something. And I said, "Well, I don't hear anything like that. Perhaps you should see your doctor? I suggest that you go to the hospital. But he said no.

"I knew from an earlier chat that he had changed his medication recently. I suspected that he might be having hallucinations.

"The next morning, I looked out my window and saw him going somewhere, I don't know where. He was wearing one of those Edmonton Oilers' t-shirts. You know, the orange jersey with the blue 'Oilers' printed on it. His hair was sticking up. I didn't hear the water running that morning, so I figured he didn't take a shower like he normally does."

"So, that was the last time you saw him, about three weeks ago?" asked Bill.

"Yes."

The officers thanked her for her time and turned to go back their car.

Off to the side of the building, beside the garbage bin, a young bottle collector about Michael's age was listening to the whole conversation. He approached them. "Ah, excuse me, officers?"

Will and Bill, and even Michael, all responded at once, "Yes?"

"I thought I saw a young guy with uncombed hair and wearing an Oilers' jersey at the gas station right across the road from here. I saw him sneak onto the back of a truck. It had an Alberta license plate number that was super easy to remember: 'LOUISE' and there was a picture of a lake on the side of the truck. I was picking bottles and cans at the time. I think it was more than a couple of weeks ago, around six or six thirty in the morning, as far as I can remember."

"Thank you for the information. May we have your first and last name, sir?" said Will.

"Leo. Leo Lightheart."

Thank you very much, Leo." Will wrote the information in his notepad and they turned to go.

But before they reached the car, Michael said to them, "Wait. I want to have a word with that witness. I'll be right back."

He walked back to the young man. "Leo, may I ask how old you are?"

"Eighteen. Why?"

"Have you heard of Karma?"

"No. Why are you asking me all these questions?"

Michael took out his wallet, opened it and handed something valuable to the bottle collector.

"A Lotto Max jackpot ticket?" exclaimed the bottle collector, as he raised his eyebrows. "I can't accept that."

"I want you to have it. If you win the ten-million-dollar Lotto Max jackpot tonight, the prize is yours. Karma is all about 'what goes around comes around.' When you're being honest, Karma will reward you with good surprises in unexpected ways, sooner or later in life."

"I'm sorry, but I value my independence. I have been on my own ever since my parents abandoned me after I was diagnosed with schizophrenia. Here, take this back. My answer is no."

"I'm sorry to hear that, but I refuse to take no for an answer. If you won't cooperate, those two police buddies of mine behind me will arrest you, big time!" threatened Michael.

Will and Bill chuckled, listening to the whole conversation.

"There's always hope that your life will change," said Michael. It could even start tonight, if you accept what is in your hand. You have to make a decision to move forward. It's either now or never. What do you say, my friend?"

"Well... Ok, I... I accept. Thank you," said Leo, as he offered his hand.

Michael and the bottle collector exchanged a firm handshake. Will and Bill exchanged smiles, as they climbed into the car.

Chapter Seventeen

It was twelve noon, by the time Mark got out of bed. He returned the family photograph to its former position on his lamp table, then went down to the dining room in a happy mood. His parents had just finished their lunch and had their running suits on.

"Your mom and I already went for a run this morning, son," said Simon. "We tried to get Buddy to come for a run with us but he wouldn't budge."

"Are you hungry?" asked Shaunabell. "There's lots of bacon and pancakes. Have a seat and eat something."

"No thank you, mom. I'm not hungry. I'm already full of energy. I feel like burning off all that fuel. Then I'll be ready to eat.

"Where's Buddy?"

"Buddy is enjoying a swim. He needs to go for a run but someone has to go with him. He can't run by himself," said Simon.

"How about I put on my running suit and go for a run with Buddy? I need to catch up with my cardiovascular exercise," said Mark.

"A great idea, son," said Simon. "But it's raining."

"I don't mind. Why not?" Mark ran outside and looked for Buddy. He saw the dog at the beach and called out his name. "Hey, Buddy! Do you want to go for a run with me?"

The dog swam to the shore and ran up to Mark.

"Let's run, Buddy!"

They began running, enjoying each other's company. Gradually, Buddy began picking up speed, speeding further and further ahead. Mark made an effort to keep up but had to stop, panting, out of breath. Buddy had completely disappeared from sight.

"I guess I'll never see you again, Buddy," Mark thought. "I might as well turn around and go back home."

As he started to turn around, he heard a strange voice. "You should appreciate your past and be grateful for the present."

Mark quickly turned around. There was a black German Shepherd. He believed it was Buddy. "Didn't I see you disappear out of sight that way?" Mark asked, pointing to the direction where he saw Buddy running.

Mark did not get a reply. So he asked, "Are you Buddy or are you a different dog?" Suddenly he realized what was going on. "Oh, I get it! You're… You're an angel! Am I right?"

"WOOF!" was the reply.

Then a bright yellow light began shining over the black German Shepherd's fur. Mark backed up a step, feeling afraid.

The dog started speaking, "I am Rebel, an angel sent by The Heavenly Creator."

"You're the one that came to the floating wooden raft where I was stranded as a child. Am I right? I thought that you were a lost dog."

"Yes, I was the one who was sent to you, my dear friend! God loves you because you're His child. God has plans for you to make miracles happen in this life.

"I'll explain, but first, let me take you to your past."

They left the present and disappeared in the bright yellow light.

Chapter Eighteen

Rebel, the angel, took Mark back to his childhood …

He was all alone, floating on a small yellow boat in the middle of a lake. He cried out for help, but nobody came.

Then he saw a dog swimming toward him. But the dog was having a lot of difficulty and it looked like it was going to drown.

Then he saw a young man swimming rapidly toward him. The man grabbed the dog and tried to lift him into the small boat. And then the man's girlfriend arrived in their boat. She helped both the man and the dog into the small boat and gave Mark one of their spare lifejackets.

Mark was scared, but the man held him on his lap. He said his name was Robert and the dog's name was Rebel.

Rebel was whimpering, exhausted. He started petting the dog.

Then the girlfriend tossed them a rope and towed the little boat back to the dock, where they were met by two police officers.

Mark remembered being terrified of the policemen at first, but then calmed down and went with them.

.

Meanwhile, Robert was still in a deep sleep, guarded by the white blue-eyed angel wolf.

He was still dreaming of hockey players in black shadows who were passing the puck to one after another with aggressive speed. The spectators around the skating rink were roaring louder and scarier. It sounded like a war was about to break out. Robert's head jerked back and forth, as the white blue-eyed angel wolf watched.

...

Rebel and Mark returned to the present and they were at the same spot on the beach from Mark's childhood.

"So, you died for me because you were an inexperienced swimmer?" asked Mark. "You were such a heroic rescuer."

"And you, Mark," said Rebel, the angel black German Shepherd. "You have a very important mission that God wants you to do right now."

"What does God want me to do?"

"Go and find Robert Ryder, the man who rescued both of us in your past. Follow a rainbow that will lead you to the forest and there you will find a bright yellow light shining on a white blue-eyed angel wolf. But you have to leave right now, before it's too late.

"Bye, now!" And with that, the angel black German Shepherd, Rebel, disappeared.

Chapter Nineteen

Mark went back to the cottage and took out his bicycle. Simon was there with Shaunabell. "Where are you going, son?" he asked.

"I just met an angel who gave me a very important mission. I have to follow a rainbow until I find a bright yellow light. That's where I will find a missing man named Robert Ryder. I've got to go, now! Bye!"

Shaunabell called after him, "Be careful when you're biking in the rain, Mark."

Mark peddled away as fast as he could.

...

Back in the forest, Robert was still in deep sleep. In his dream, the hockey players were aggressively passing the puck back and forth. The spectators were getting louder and scarier than ever. Robert's head jerked faster and faster.

The white blue-eyed angel wolf was still standing there, guarding the lost man

...

Meanwhile, Simon received a call from his air ambulance crew about the search for the missing man by the name of Robert Ryder. Simon quickly went to his room and changed into his paramedic uniform.

Shaunabell also changed and got ready to help with the search.

...

In Edmonton, two helicopters took off on emergency flights. One was an RCMP chopper, with a pilot and Robert's brother, RCMP constable Dave Ryder. The other transported a paramedic and his pilot. They were heading to Lake Louise to join in the search for the missing man.

...

Mark was about halfway there, following the rainbow down the quiet highway.

...

Back in the forest, in Robert's deep dream, the spectators were starting to get out of control. The aggressive puck passing was causing Robert's head to jerk crazily back and forth.

...

Finally, the rainbow that Mark was following ended. He could see a bright yellow light shining in through the forest.

"This is where the missing man must be," thought Mark. "I'll go down along the ditch and check it out."

While Mark was walking his bike along the ditch, he noticed shoe prints in the mud. He followed them to a tree branch, where he saw specks of blood. He guessed that Robert's leg must have been scratched by sharp twigs. "He's in here somewhere," thought Mark.

He took out his phone and snapped a picture of the blood and another picture of the highway speed limit sign that showed the highway number. He texted them individually to each of his parents.

…

Back at the cottage, Simon and Shaunabell looked at the photos and immediately realized exactly where Mark was. Simon forwarded the message to the air ambulance paramedic. A minute later, Constable Dave Ryder received the text message from the air ambulance paramedic.

…

Mark kept following the bright yellow light, until he saw the wolf standing guard over the sleeping man.

When he looked more closely, he could see that the man's head was jerking back and forth. He noticed specks of blood on his ankle and shin and he could see the Oilers' T-shirt that Robert was wearing. Mark snapped a picture of the sleeping man with the identifying clothes on.

Mark took out his iPhone from his hoodie pocket and phoned his father.

Simon answered with the speaker on, so that Shaunabell would be able to hear the whole conversation. "Yes, Mark?"

Mark explained, "Dad, I found the missing man! He's wearing an Oiler's T-shirt and I see specks of blood on his leg ---"

Simon interrupted. "I already received your texts and I forwarded them to the rescue party. So, tell me more about what's happening there."

Mark said, "This guy's head is jerking back and forth out of control. His eyes are closed and he doesn't seem to be aware that I'm standing here."

"Is there anything else?" asked Simon.

Mark was looking at the angel wolf, wondering whether or not he should tell his father. The wolf could sense that Mark was unsure, so he barked loudly, "WOOF!"

"Did that bark come from a white blue-eyed wolf?" demanded Simon.

"Yes, Dad. But he seems harmless. He's just standing here beside me."

"Good! Then there's nothing to be afraid of. Now, tell me exactly where you are."

"I'm in the middle of the woods near a pond. The woods that I'm in are near the highway, about one hour by bike from the cottage. The speed limit on the sign near where I left my bike says 60 kilometres per hour. That's where you can find me."

Shaunabell checked on Google Maps and found the exact spot where the pond was located. She texted the map to Simon and he forwarded it to the rescue party.

"Mark, just stay where you are," Simon ordered. "Rescue is on the way. Do not touch the sleeping man or make any loud noise. Understood?"

"Understood."

"Bye for now," Simon hung up right away. "Let's go, Shaunabell!"

Simon and Shaunabell climbed into their blue truck. Simon started the engine and off they went to meet with the rescue party at the location Mark had given them.

Chapter Twenty

Inside Robert's head, the roar from the spectators at the arena was getting louder and scarier than ever. The players were passing the puck even faster and Robert's head twitched even faster.

Mark and the white wolf just stood there, watching. Then the wolf sensed the arrival of the rescue party and ran off, leaving Mark alone.

By the time Simon and Shaunabell arrived a few minutes later, the rescue party had identified the sleeping man as the Robert Ryder they had been searching for.

...

In Robert's dream, the skating rink melted in a violent tsunami that flung the puck into the air with such force that it flew all the way up to the highest seat where he was standing. It hit him in the face and his eyebrow started to bleed.

The sleeping man woke up, freaking out in front of everyone. "OUCH! I got hit in the eye by a hockey puck. It's bleeding real bad!"

"Robert, there's no cut or blood on your eyebrow," said his brother, the RCMP constable.

Robert began talking rapidly. "I was just watching a hockey game. There were shadowy hockey players who were very aggressively passing the puck back and forth.

Then the ice all melted and a puck flew at me and hit me in the face and cut my eyebrow! Then I—"

"Robert! Robert! You were just hallucinating and dreaming," said the Dave. "Get up, now! You're flying to the hospital back to Edmonton with the air ambulance paramedics."

Robert climbed slowly to his feet. He looked around and then asked, "Ah, where's the white blue-eyed wolf that was standing here guarding me?"

"Never mind that!" said Paramedic Simon. "Come with me, Robert! We don't have all day! And you, Mark, you'll have to fly with the RCMP back to Edmonton. We have no room for you in the air ambulance."

Robert hopped on the air ambulance helicopter with paramedic Simon, while Mark climbed aboard the other helicopter with the RCMP. Then both helicopters took off and headed back to Edmonton.

Shaunabell put Mark's bike in the truck and drove off to Edmonton to meet with everyone at the local hospital.

...

The Previous Night:

It was nine PM. Someone was knocking on the door of the restaurant where the manager was switching off the lights. The manager saw two strangers outside at the front door and wondered what they wanted. So, he went and opened the door.

"Yes, may I help you?"

"Sorry, to bother you at this time of the night." It was a homeless man and woman. "My wife and I want to show you this picture of us with our five-year-old son. It was taken here thirteen years ago on March 22nd, his fifth birthday."

The manager took a close look. He saw a five-year-old boy with dark curly hair, holding a pencil. There were a stack of papers on a restaurant table and a young father with dark curly hair and a young mother with strong cheek bones, holding a medical book in her hand. In the background there were tables full of customers. Right away, the manager recognized the background. The little boy looked familiar.

"That boy with the dark curly hair looks just like one of my eighteen-year-old employees. The table looks like one of my restaurant tables. Are you familiar with this place?"

"Yes, I am," said the homeless man. "I used to work there as a dining room manager until I lost my position due to mental health issues."

"May I ask for your name?" said the manager.

"It's Mark Brown," replied the homeless man.

"One of my employees has the same first name as you. I expect that one day he'll get a promotion to manager."

"That sounds like the guy my wife and I met a few hours ago. He fed us hotdogs and iced tea and chocolate chip cookies!"

"I met his parents only once," said the manager. "He doesn't look like either of them. He... he actually looks a lot like you. He has the same dark curly hair. And you, ma'am, he has your cheekbones!"

The homeless man began stuttering. "Your employee must be our... our..."

"MY BABY! MY BABY!" cried the homeless woman. She collapsed on the floor still crying, "MY BABY! MY BABY!"

Suddenly, the homeless man also collapsed – he had suffered a heart attack and lost consciousness.

The restaurant manager grabbed his phone and dialed 911. Then he emailed Simon and Shaunabell to tell them how their son's biological parents had reacted when they learned about Mark.

Simon replied immediately that he would call an air ambulance to transport them both to the local hospital in Edmonton.

Chapter Twenty-One

At the hospital, Robert was admitted and taken by wheelchair to the blood lab. Mark was already lying on a bed, getting ready to transfuse Rebel's One-of-a-kind Miracle Blood into Robert's arm.

...

After the transfusion, Robert was given a powerful sleeping pill. Then he was wheeled to a dark room with closed curtains, in the psychiatric unit. He immediately fell asleep in the comfortable bed.

...

Robert woke up naturally, feeling a bit groggy. He saw the nurse holding a needle in her hand and realized he was getting a blood test.

"I had a very, very long dream," said Robert. "How long have I been sleeping?"

"Two weeks," replied the nurse.

"Are you serious? How could I have slept that long?

"Your doctor will explain it to you after breakfast. But first, I need to take a blood sample. Hold still and relax."

...

After Robert finished his breakfast, a nurse brought him to a consulting room, where the doctor and a medical student were waiting.

"Good morning, Robert. I'm Dr. Brian Larry James, your psychiatrist," said the doctor. "You can call me Dr. James. And this is Darren, my medical student."

Robert smiled and shook hands with them.

"That's a nice firm handshake and a confident smile," said Dr. James. "We're impressed. Please have a seat.

"Now, before we begin, we want you to take this notepad and write down any questions you have."

Robert took the notepad and wrote, "What did you inject into my arm at the blood lab?"

Dr. James read the question and turned to his student. "Notice Robert's neat handwriting."

Turning to Robert, he said, "We transfused you with blood from an eighteen-year-old donor. It contains a cure for your psychological condition. We call the cure, 'Rebel's one-of-a-kind Miracle Blood.'

The doctor went on to explain how the cure had been discovered in the blood of a deceased dog thirteen years earlier at Lake Louise.

"I recognize the dog's name. That was the half-wolf and half German Shepherd dog that died in Lake Louise back then," said Robert. "Am I the first to receive this cure?"

"Well, yes and no," answered Dr. James.

"I don't understand," said Robert.

Dr. James then told Robert the whole story of how the dog had died after attempting to rescue the young boy on the raft and how the scientist, Dr. Pierre Royal Mackenzie, working in his top-secret lab, had collected the blood and discovered how it could improve the quality of life for people with schizophrenia and bipolar disorder.

He explained how the young boy had been diagnosed with schizophrenia and how they gave him a transfusion of the special blood. He finished by pointing out that they had been observing the boy for the last thirteen years, to make sure it worked properly to keep him in touch with reality.

"You received a transfusion from that boy," said the doctor. "We expect it to keep you from having symptoms, but we will want to meet with you again in two weeks to do a checkup."

"That's it for this meeting, bye for now and see you in two weeks."

"Bye, doctor. Bye, Darren," said Robert with a big sigh of relief.

Chapter Twenty-Two

Two days after flying his son and the missing man to Edmonton, Simon and his team received a call about a woman who was screaming loudly enough that everyone in the apartment building could hear her.

The team arrived to discover a violent scene in the woman's living room. A young woman was holding a chair and threatening a young man.

"Get out of my apartment, Dax! You're not registered with the landlord! What you're doing is illegal!"

Paramedic Simon recognized the young woman – she worked with her son at the restaurant. He called to her as he slowly approached. "Hey, hey, hey! Lynnora, what's going on?"

Lynnora recognized him. "Simon? Mark's dad? Oh, Simon, am I ever glad you're here!"

Simon hugged her and tried to console her. "Tell us what's going on. There's nothing to be afraid of."

Through her sobs, Lynnora told the story of what her abusive boyfriend had been putting her through. She explained that she became violent after her bipolar disorder medication was changed.

The paramedic team could see cigarette butts everywhere; in the living room, dining room, and washroom. They saw empty cans of beer all over the counter in the kitchen and a fridge full of beer, but no food or other beverages.

One of the paramedics asked Dax if he had a full-time job and was helping with the rent. Dax claimed that his mother paid the rent, but they didn't believe his story, and decided to notify the police.

The police had already been called and arrived a few minutes later. After hearing the story, they arrested Dax for trespassing, since he was not registered with the property owner as a tenant.

Simon called Dr. James and explained the situation. He asked them to bring the woman in to the hospital for further tests.

Simon and the team escorted the woman to the air ambulance and took off immediately for Edmonton.

Once Lynnora was admitted as an inpatient at the hospital, she was immediately given a transfusion of Rebel's One-of-a-kind Miracle Blood. She was given a strong sleeping pill and moved into the same unit where Robert was recovering.

Chapter Twenty-Three

Down the hall from Lynnora's room, in the hospital beauty salon, there was a sudden, loud piercing scream. Two security guards ran quickly down the hallway to the salon, where they found the salon manager screaming at her employee, a woman with a weird, colourful peacock-looking hairstyle, "BUBBLE, I HIRED YOU THIS MORNING WITH HIGH CONFIDENCE EVEN THOUGH YOU HAVE A BAD REPUTATION AND A HISTORY OF GETTING FIRED FROM EVERY SINGLE BEAUTY SALON ACROSS ALL OF NORTH AMERICA FOR YOUR GUMSNAPPING! AND YOU KNOW WHAT? YOU'RE FIRED AGAIN!"

The screaming, out-of-control manager was restrained by the security guards and other emergency room workers. They gave her a sedative and admitted her as a patient.

...

Three days later, the manager was diagnosed with bipolar disorder and given a transfusion of Rebel's One-of-a-kind Miracle Blood. She was sedated and wheeled into the same ward where Robert and Lynnora were sleeping.

...

Mark became a hospital resident for life. His full-time job: providing transfusion of the miracle blood, five days a week.

Chapter Twenty-Four

Two weeks later, Lynnora woke up slowly, feeling groggy. She saw the nurse and asked, "Ah, nurse? I just had a very, very long dream. How long have I been in bed sleeping?"

"Two peaceful weeks, Lynnora."

"That long?"

"Yes," replied the nurse. Now, just relax while I take a blood sample."

Lynnora never felt anything as the nurse took blood from her arm. "You're done, now. Another nurse will take you to meet with the doctor. But first, you should head to the dining room and have some breakfast."

Lynnora went to the dining room and sat down at a table with a crowd of patients, and ate her breakfast.

When she was finished, a nurse came in to take her to a private meeting room.

As she entered, she saw two men in the room. "Good morning, Lynnora," said one with a smile. I'm Dr. Brian Larry James, your psychiatrist. You can call me Dr. James."

"Good morning, Dr. James," said Lynnora, returning the smile with a firm handshake.

"And this is Darren, my medical student." said Dr. James.

Darren and Lynnora exchanged smiles and handshakes.

"Another firm handshake from a second patient — that's two in a row so far!" said the two men to each other. They sat down at the table.

Dr. James asked her if bipolar disorder ran in her family. Lynnora told them that one of the siblings on her mother's side of the family had bipolar disorder and that she believed it may have been inherited from her grandparents.

He then asked if there were any cases on her father's side of the family. She explained that her father was an only child and that he had passed away from a heart attack when she was a young child. She was raised by her mother and didn't know anything else about her father.

Lynnora volunteered what she went through when her ex-boyfriend and his drinking/smoking buddies would come over and eat all the food in the fridge and not even pitch in to help with the rent. They would party all night and keep her awake, and then she had to go to work, tired and stressed out.

She had no money left after the boyfriend and his buddies spent it all on cigarettes and beer, but she had difficulties standing up for her rights.

Dr. James asked her for permission to communicate with her mother as next-of-kin and Lynnora signed the permission form.

Then their private meeting was over. Dr. James scheduled another meeting in two weeks.

Chapter Twenty-Five

The hair salon manager woke up feeling groggy and saw a nurse standing over her. "Where am I? And how long have I been sleeping?"

"You are in the hospital," answered the nurse. "You've been unconscious for almost two weeks."

"Two fricken' weeks! So, I'm a hospital patient instead of a hospital hair salon manager! Thanks a lot to that silly gumsnapping employee. She ruined my beautiful long hair when she deliberately spat bubblegum on it!"

She reached up to smooth her hair, but she touched the top of her head and realized that she was bald! "Now, I'm bald headed!" she cried. "Who shaved my head?"

"One of the nurses did it while you were sleeping, because your hair was such a disaster. Now, relax while I collect blood from your arm, okay?"

...

In the meeting room, Dr. James and Darren asked the salon manager if bipolar disorder ran in her family. She thought for a few minutes and then finally remembered. Her great grandmother on her father's side had passed away in Germany from a rare mental illness two weeks before her thirtieth birthday. It had a strange name that they had never heard before and she was able to remember the name, "Hitler's Mania."

Dr. James did a computer search for the rare disease on his laptop. According to the search results, the disease could have a number of serious symptoms:

- dangerous risk taking
- confrontational behaviour
- impulsive decision making
- irrational and bizarre revenge teasing
- always needing to have the last word in a conversation.

Individuals with this rare disease are talented in water safety, but sadly, they die before age thirty.

The salon manager's heart was racing and she was feeling very emotional. But Dr. James said that she was lucky because she didn't inherit that rare disease.

She explained that her family doctor recommended that she avoid getting pregnant, because it would be too dangerous to pass on the rare disease to the baby. He suggested that she raise wolves and German Shepherds instead.

Since the name, 'Rebel's One-of-a-kind Miracle Blood' sounded familiar, she mentioned that she was an animal breeder and how her pet, Rebel, was born as a mixed wolf-German Shepherd.

Dr. James and Darren were surprised! They were actually meeting Rebel's animal breeder right there in the meeting room.

They explained about their experiment with her and the two patients before her. Suddenly, everything made sense. She felt blessed when she realized that there was a purpose for her in her life.

Dr. James thanked her for coming to the meeting and made an appointment in two weeks.

A nurse walked into the room and announced, "There is a very important news story you should watch."

The salon manager started to worry, wondering what the new was about and why it concerned her.

...

On the television, the newswoman was speaking with the authorities. In the background was a house by a lake. "Two weeks ago, in Lake Louise, a very expensive modern property home was totally destroyed by lightning. The previous owner, Rihanna Valentine, had done extensive renovations before selling it. The property was valued at the high end of the market after it was purchased by a generous, wealthy investor."

The salon manager recognized the destroyed property. "That used to be my home! Now it has been destroyed!" cried Rihanna Valentine. "I could've been killed by lightning!"

Rihanna was so upset she turned the TV off and left the room, and went straight to bed for a nap.

Chapter Twenty-Six

That evening, Rihanna was awakened by a knock on her door. "Yes?" she called.

"You have a visitor here to see you," said the nurse. "She's at the nurse's desk."

Rihanna got out of bed and went to meet her visitor. She immediately recognized her. "Hi, Pam!" she said, feeling much better. She was getting over the news she heard earlier.

"Hi, Rihanna!" said Pam with a friendly smile. "Long time no see! Last time was at my dog's funeral! I've been thinking of you ever since Bubble showed up at home so early from work. I have a gift here in my shopping bag that you'll appreciate. How have you been?"

"I was emotional this morning," said Rihanna. "Let's have a seat in the dining room."

"Sure, I'll join you!"

They sat down at a table and started talking.

"I've heard on news about the house that I sold in Lake Louise that was destroyed by lightning," said Rihanna. "I feel that she deserves all her money back, as well as the beauty salon that she gave me for free."

"I don't want the salon any more. I can't forget how Bubble purposely spat bubblegum all over my hair. I had to have it cut off and now it looks terrible."

"Yes, I can see that," said Pam.

"That behaviour is not normal," said Rihanna. "Bubble must be suffering from a mental disorder. She needs help."

"I agree," said Pam. "There's one thing I noticed. It's about how Bubble responds to teasing. You know what my daughter Elaine is like. She likes to bug her about her job, with questions like, 'Why do you cut hair for a living? What's so important about hair? It's a stupid business!' And of course, Elaine always has the last word.

"So Bubble gets angry, like a pre-teen and she says things like, 'It is not a stupid business! I like it!'"

"She does, eh?" asked Rihanna. "So, what does Elaine do, nowadays?"

"Nowadays, Elaine is a lifeguard. She's twenty-five now," said Pam. "But, before that, she got suspended two weeks before her graduation from the Navy Seals because she blew up at the Sergeant. She made threats against him in front of the whole crew. The whole family was very disappointed in her, especially me!"

"I don't blame you."

"And it wasn't the first time," Pam continued. "One time back in grade six, Elaine got suspended for three days. She got into a fight with one of her classmates who asked her, 'Elaine, are you a boy?' That happened after Elaine had to cut her hair off because Aunt Bubble got bubblegum in it.

"Elaine even jeopardized our gym memberships and my business when she confronted some punks for making insulting comments about how well developed my physique was.

"She used her judo skills on them, including a foot sweep that was strictly forbidden by her black belt judo instructor. Then she blocked the woman punk's punch and almost crushed her hand. I had to abandon the client I was training and stop that aggressive kid of mine.

"And, Elaine confronted her CPR instructor after she was accused of cheating on her final exam. I was notified by the school while I was in the middle of training a client, and I had to show up and take over the responsibility of having a serious conversation with that troubled student who happens to be my kid—my only kid! At least, she would settle down after I got through to her.

"Then there was the time that she overheard me talking about her half-sister. She threatened to disown me and gave me attitude all week, by not speaking with me or sitting with me at the breakfast table.

"Finally, I couldn't tolerate that type of behaviour anymore and I sent her to a beach camp where other troubled teenagers are sent for professional counselling, like to overcome death in the family. She eventually learned the truth about her half-sister, Elizabeth, and at that point I gave her up to be under her sister's legal custody, so that she could further her education in a military school.

"Elaine still hasn't changed; in fact, she got worse when she had to put down her two mixed German Shepherd-and-Husky dogs – you know, the ones you sold to her when you and I first met, after I responded to your ad.

"I even introduced Elizabeth to you and she bought one of your pure-bred German Shepherds."

"I remember," said Rihanna. "Speaking of Elizabeth, how come she adopted one pure-bred German Shepherd instead of a mixed-breed dog?"

"Elizabeth is fussy about mixed breed animals," said Pam. "According to her father's information, she got that from her mother."

Rihanna was thinking …

Elaine's irrational behaviour was similar to how Rihanna's great grandmother had behaved. Perhaps Elaine is suffering from the same rare disease that her great grandmother died from, two weeks before her thirtieth birthday. But how could she tell that to Pam without scaring her?

"Ummm, Pam, how old is Elaine now?" asked Rihanna.

"Twenty five. Why?"

"Just making sure," said Rihanna with deep concern.

"May I ask what's on your mind?" asked Pam, wondering what made Rihanna bring up that question.

Before Rihanna could reply, the nurse approached their table, announcing that visiting hours were over.

Pam quickly said goodbye to Rihanna and handed her the shopping bag, with a heavy box in it for her to keep.

Rihanna went back to her room and sat down on her bed. She unwrapped the heavy box, wondering what it could be. To her surprise it was a porcelain statue of her puppy, Rebel the half-wolf-and-half-German Shepherd!

Rihanna felt touched and started to cry. "Oh, thank you so much! I really appreciate it!" Rihanna said out loud.

There were also some photographs:

One photograph was of the whole family:
Pam Williams, her daughter Elaine, and her stepdaughter, Elizabeth Johnson.

There were three more individual photographs:

- Pam Williams with her two half-wolf-and-half-German Shepherds.
- Elaine and her two mixed bred German Shepherd / Husky dogs.
- Elizabeth and her one and only purebred German Shepherd.

Rihanna was very thankful. She placed the porcelain statue by the window, laid down and was soon sleeping happily.

Chapter Twenty-Seven

Four weeks later …

Dr. James and Darren walked down the hallway, having a business conversation. As they passed the chapel, they heard someone singing. They opened the door, quietly and saw it was one of their patients —Rihanna!

Rihanna was singing so beautifully in a normal tone. Her song was about how she perceived reality.

The two men listened for at least five minutes. They thought that Rihanna's singing was amazing!

"This means that 'Rebel's One-of-a-kind Miracle Blood' is doing the job," said Dr. James.

Rihanna finished her song and knelt down and began praying. Dr. James and Darren left the chapel to continue to their meeting, quietly closing the door, so that they didn't disturb the patient.

Chapter Twenty-Eight

The next day, Rihanna, Lynnora, and Robert were given a short story to read, and were asked to write an essay comparing the composition to reality. They had until the next day to complete their assignments.

The following day, they handed their assignments to a medical student who, in turn, handed them over to the psychiatrist and scientist, so they could add to their study on the viability of Rebel's One-of-a-kind Miracle Blood.

Then the three patients were given a second assignment: make a photo collage to explain how each one of them perceives reality.

Rihanna went first: "I have a photograph from a magazine that shows me walking slowly on a narrow bridge high above a waterfall between two mountain cliffs. There are no handrails to hold onto for support. A white blue-eyed wolf is following me. I call it 'Life Is A Personal, Risky, Coin-Toss Journey.'

"I had a choice: either I escape from the hostile environment where I was being held by dangerous criminals with the two pets I was adopting, or let them destroy both the Luna wolf and the German Shepherd. I don't know why they were holding us. The long narrow bridge was the only way out. The three of us snuck out of there in the dark, quietly, when everyone was sleeping.

"I had trained the two dogs way ahead of time on how to escape without barking. We walked for miles until three o'clock in the morning, when we reached the beginning of the narrow bridge. We could hear the sound of the waterfall.

"The Luna wolf was calm, due to her wild nature, but the German Shepherd was whimpering. He sounded scared and unsure of the risky escape, especially in the wild nature that he unaccustomed to. I made a deal with him that his female mate and I would walk together by ourselves all the way to the other end and then wait for him to walk across.

"So, anyway, the Luna wolf followed behind me, one step at a time on the long bridge. I could no longer focus on who was behind me, but I wished the Luna wolf good luck. The only one I had to focus on was myself — I was on my own at my own risk.

"I took my time step by step with faithfulness, listening to the loud sounds of the waterfall. I was a bit nervous but I kept on going, relying on my own two feet, keeping my balance steady. It felt that it was going to take forever to make it to safety. I had to keep focusing on every single step I took, without looking too far ahead, otherwise I would've lost my balance then I would've been doomed. Finally, I took my last step and I was safe on the other mountain cliff. I let out a big sigh — I was relieved!

"Then the Luna wolf made it too. That was another relief! Then we waited for the German Shepherd but he had disappeared!

"Two months later, on the 27th of May, the Luna wolf had a litter of four puppies. They were born in a den in the mountains at Lake Louise where we were camping. I felt so proud of being a second mother to them. I was quite surprised that the Luna wolf was pregnant! I always knew that the father must've been the German Shepherd. I mean, who else could the Luna wolf be mating with, since they were the only two on that property with me? So that German Shepherd had to be the father! I mean, all the puppies look part German Shepherd.

"One morning as I was coming home with a pail of fresh water from the river, I spotted two women that I recognized, stealing the mother wolf and the newborn puppies. I shouted, 'Hey, you thieves!'

"Then they quickly spun around. And I said, 'Keep your bloody hands off my family, or else!' I dropped the pail of water and started charging towards them.

"They took off with the wolf and puppies. But a car came out of nowhere and the two criminals jumped into the car with my wolf family and they took off. I shouted at them before they were out of earshot, 'I'm ready for the next challenge next time we meet! Nobody messes around with a VALENTINE!'

"I went back to where I had left the pail of fresh water, feeling very upset. But then, I saw a little one drinking water in the pail. It was one of my puppies — my puppy son! The only boy in the family! I wondered to myself, 'How did this little one manage to escape from those dangerous criminals?' I had no idea how this one survived. He's my miracle puppy son, so I named him Rebel. That's the only 'R' name I could think of after me. I kept Rebel and took him to my home in Lake Louise.

"I raised Rebel with powerful love, until I sold him to an Edmonton family when he was two months old. I didn't want to sell him, but I was eight hundred dollars short after starting my own business as an animal breeder. But at least he went to a home where he was protected from those dangerous criminals.

"That's my story. In conclusion, this photograph that I call, 'Life Is A Personal, Risky, Coin-Toss Journey' is how I perceive reality."

"That's the most amazing story I have ever heard, Rihanna!" said Dr. James. "I'm quite thrilled how you've survived through all this!"

Then he turned his attention to Lynnora. "How about you, Lynnora? Tell us how you perceive reality."

"Well, here's my painting of mountains full of ice cream, desserts, and coffee beans. I call it, 'Faith Can Move Mountains.'

"That's how I perceive reality. In this world, I can make an impossibility into a possibility, just by having faith in myself. For example, in my job, I want to work my way up from a dishwasher to a coffee shop owner.

"I suppose that our big cake with the name 'Rebel's One-of-a-kind Miracle Blood' on it and our pot of coffee must've given you that idea of wanting to become a coffee and dessert shop owner. Am I correct?"

"You betcha, Dr. James!" Lynnora said, feeling optimistic.

"Well, anything is possible if you focus your mind on it, Lynnora," Dr. James chuckled. "I'll support your goal and wish you good luck!"

Then he turned his attention to Robert. "Now, it's your turn, Robert. Tell us how you perceive reality."

"Well, here's a colouring of a hockey stick and puck with the motto, 'Life's A Game.' That's how I perceive reality. In the real world I no longer take things personally or straight to the heart.

"For example, one of the patients that I made friends with never bothered to say goodbye to me when he was discharged. Right away, I realized that it has nothing to do with me. I'm not the only patient he wanted nothing to do with. I mean, patients come and go. He just wanted to move on with his life and doesn't want to keep in touch with me, because I remind him of the hospital.

"Well, that's just part of the game. Sometimes you win, sometimes you lose – 'Life's A Game.'"

"That makes sense, Robert," said Dr. James. "That's a fact of life. Friends come and go. Also, friends outgrow each other sometimes. It has nothing to do with you. Anyway, do you have anything else to share with us, Robert?"

"Yes, I do," said Robert. "There's something that I want to volunteer to the group. It's about my dog, Rebel, that I lost thirteen years ago."

Rihanna recognized the name and started paying close attention.

Robert continued his story, "I raised Rebel for the last six months before he died. At first, I had a phobia of dogs, but then I overcame it one night when I had to take over the responsibilities of taking care of him without my parents' supervision. I had Rebel all to myself when my parents moved away for work. It required a lot of patience, which wasn't easy.

"Eventually, I introduced Rebel to the girl I was dating. At first, he didn't accept her, but after a while they became friends. The three of us went on a one-week vacation to Lake Louise ,and one day, when we were swimming from the boat in the middle of the lake, we heard him barking. By the time we got back to the boat, Rebel was swimming out to where a little boy was stranded on a small boat.

"We rescued the little boy, but Rebel was worn out. Even though he had no swimming experience, he attempted to save that little boy's life, at his own risk.

"After we got back to Edmonton, we took him to the vet. His condition was getting worse.

"The test results were sad news. Rebel had only two days left to live. We took him back home where he could live out his remaining days, where he was familiar with the environment.

"To make a long story short, we ended up being held hostage by a criminal. We had a fight, but somehow the house caught fire. Rebel ran to get help from a guy who turned out to be my long-lost brother, Dave, the one who used to tease me. But Dave was also taken hostage.

"Just as the criminal pulled a gun, Rebel came flying through the window and started attacking the criminal. We escaped, but once we were free, Rebel came up to me, lay down between my brother and me, then he… then he… he died! He died for my brother and I -- for our reunion!"

Robert broke down and cried, feeling very emotional. And so did Rihanna. She reached for Robert's hand and said, "That was my puppy who became your heroic dog, Robert."

Lynnora reached for both of them and held their hands. After a moment, she spoke up, "That dog was a miracle. As a result of Rebel's blood, I'm a hundred percent back in reality now. Thank you, both of you, for taking such great care of Rebel. Both of you deserve credit."

"There's one more person to thank, and all of you will be meeting him on Thanksgiving Day," said Dr. James.

Chapter Twenty-Nine

On Thanksgiving Day, after breakfast, all three patients went to see Dr. James and his student, to hear what the scientist had to say about their results from their essays and art projects.

"Good morning, Robert, Rihanna, and Lynnora," greeted Dr. James with a smile. "This gentleman with me here has a surprising announcement to make." He turned to his guest and said, "Please go ahead."

"Good morning, everyone! My name is Dr. Pierre Royal Mackenzie. I have been studying your case histories and I examined all your essays and your art projects very carefully. All your results are very positive!

"That means 'Rebel's One-of-a-kind Miracle Blood' is successful in providing a better quality-of-life for bipolar disorder and schizophrenia sufferers! Congratulations!" Dr. Pierre Royal Mackenzie had a big cheerful smile on his face.

"Wow! I don't believe this! I'm a person with confidence for the very first time in my life!" said Robert, sounding happy.

"Me too!" said Rihanna. "My highs and lows are over! Even my singing tone is at the right level!"

"Dr. James and Darren mentioned that your tone in singing has very much improved after hearing you singing a song about how you perceive reality."

"Really?" asked Rihanna.

Dr. James, Darren, and Dr. Mackenzie smiled in reply.

"Me, most!" said Lynnora. "I'm no longer gullible! I don't allow anyone to walk all over me nowadays. I have the backbone to take care of my own battles!"

"And now, all of us are free from those diseases because of 'Rebel's One-of-a-kind Miracle Blood'" said all three patients with confidence.

Chapter Thirty

After the meeting, Robert sat alone in the dining room having a cup of coffee. Suddenly he heard a tapping sound on the window behind him. He turned around and recognized the white blue-eyed wolf that was looking at him through the window.

"What are you doing here?" said Robert. "Go back home to Lake Louise where you came from! Just go before people see you!"

To Robert's surprise, a bright yellow light started to shine on the wolf's head and shoulders. Robert backed away a step asking, "Who are you?"

The wolf began speaking inside Robert's mind, "I am Rebel, an angel sent by The Heavenly Creator. God loves you because you're His child. God is very proud of you for surviving your hallucinations and the three-week starvation when you were lost in the woods.

"You also successfully received a transfusion of Rebel's One-of-a-kind Miracle Blood and now there will be no more paranoia, silly thoughts or imaginations or inappropriate behaviour. You'll now be able to live with yourself.

"You were dreaming about a hockey game while I was guarding you in the forest near Lake Louise. Life can be a little wild sometimes. After all, Life's A Game. You have come a long way, Robert! God is rewarding you!" And then the wolf disappeared.

Chapter Thirty-One

The cafeteria was full of visitors for Thanksgiving Day lunch. Pam, Rihanna's visitor, had already left for business in California. Robert and Lynnora were in the lineup buying a piece of the cake that was decorated with a red capital 'R' to celebrate 'Rebel's One-of-a-kind Miracle Blood.'

"I'll catch up with you, Robert," said Lynnora when it was her turn to purchase her item.

Lynnora wondered out loud, "Who is the creator of this incredible cake?"

"I am, young lady," said a strange voice behind her.

Lynnora was startled and said, as she turned around, "You're the one that came up with such an amazing recipe?"

"Yep!"

"Just hold on for a moment ,while I finish purchasing this creation of yours."

Lynnora purchased her cake and turned back to the stranger and held out her hand. "I'm Lynnora, a patient from the West unit."

"I'm Leo, a patient from the East unit," he said as he shook her hand.

"Come and join me and my friends and parents at my table," Lynnora invited.

"Sure, I would love to!"

At the table sat Robert, his RCMP constable brother, Dave, his nephew, Michael, her mother, stepfather and two police officer friends of Robert's. Before Lynnora had a chance to introduce him, they all recognized him and said, "Hi, Leo! Is that your new girlfriend?"

Everybody chuckled.

Lynnora was surprised. "You guys know each other?"

"Yes," said Robert. "Leo was the witness who saw me when I climbed in the back of somebody's truck so I could get to Lake Louise."

"And Robert's nephew gave me his Lotto Max ticket as a reward," said Leo. He taught me about Karma: 'What goes around comes around.' And that night I actually won! Well, half of the prize!"

"These two police officers, Will and Bill claimed the prize for me and set up a savings account under my name. I no longer have to worry about collecting bottles and cans for survival. I'm now independent. I already bought a condo and I'm opening up my very own coffee shop. My whole life has changed."

"You said you won half of the jackpot. Who was the other winner?" asked Lynnora.

"Ummm…Oh, now I remember," said Leo. "According to the news, they're looking for a young woman who purchased a Lotto Max ticket at Lake Louise. Why?"

"Excuse me," said Lynnora. "I'll be right back."

Lynnora left the table and went to the washroom for privacy. She opened her purse and pulled out a Lotto Max ticket. She had completely forgotten about it, until Leo mentioned his win. She took out her iPhone, dialed the Lotto Max line and listened to the recording. She took a look at her ticket -- all seven numbers and the exact date of the day of the draw -- they all matched! She listened to the recording three more times, just to be sure. Lynnora could not believe that she was the jackpot winner! She began jumping up and down for joy!

"I'm the winner! I'm the winner!" But then she told herself, "I must remain calm in public."

Lynnora returned to the cafeteria right away and approached Constable Dave. "Excuse me, Constable Dave. Sorry to interrupt your conversation. Can I talk to you in private? It's urgent."

"Of course," Dave turned to the others. "Excuse me for a moment."

Lynnora and Constable Dave went outside, where no one could hear them. "Look," said Lynnora. Then she showed him her Lotto Max jackpot ticket.

Constable Dave took a look at the ticket. He pulled out his iPhone and dialed the Lotto Max line just to triple check, and then smiled. He knew exactly why Lynnora had approached him.

"Come with me, Lynnora," he said. "I'm taking you to claim the prize. I'll take care of everything! Let's go!" and off they went to the Lotto Max Center, where Dave helped Lynnora go through the whole claim process.

Chapter Thirty-Two

Back in the cafeteria, Rihanna could hear a conversation between a homeless couple and the Barker family. She was interested in what they had to say.

Simon was speaking to Mark. "Here are the two people you fed at your place of work. Can you figure out what their real relationship is to you?"

"Yes, I already figured it out from what you said about my own past."

He turned to the woman. "When we were speaking behind the restaurant, you mentioned that you had graduated at the top of your class at age twelve. And, you mentioned that you have a degree in medicine. Well, same here. I graduated at fifteen and I'm already accepted to study medicine."

Then Mark turned his attention to the man. "And you said that you were a top-level dining room manager. Well, I'm a top full-time waiter. It runs in the family — Mom and Dad!"

The three of them jumped up from the table and hugged each other, letting out a big group sigh.

"It's a miracle that God answered our prayers after thirteen long years. And all because of that black German Shepherd who brought us back into your life, after he approached us at the park where we were sleeping," said his long-lost parents.

"How did the both of you end up here?" Mark wanted to know.

"Your dad will tell you all about it, Mark," said his birth father.

Simon began telling Mark the story about how his birth parents were found:

"That night when you took off, I had an email from your boss. He said that two homeless people, Mark and Mary Brown had claimed to be your birth parents, but they had both collapsed from exhaustion.

"I recognized their names right away and I recommended that they were to be air-ambulanced here. I arranged each of them a bed for their own medical safety.

"And now, they have regained a sense of reality because of a transfusion of 'Rebel's One-of-a-kind Miracle Blood'. You weren't aware of them when the transfusion was done. Now they are back to normal and they are moving on with their lives in the real world just like you are."

"Son?" said Mark senior.

"Yes, Dad?"

"Will you forgive me for abandoning you on the yellow rubber boat when you were five?"

"Of course, Dad," said Mark junior. "That's water under the bridge."

They hugged each other. Mark senior was in tears and feeling guilty for his past actions.

Chapter Thirty-Three

"I understand that you are a 'Rebel's One-of-a-kind Miracle Blood' transfuser for a life," said Mark senior. "And who was the person who bred Rebel, the half-wolf-and-half-German Shepherd that died for you after you were rescued by him? I would like to meet that person."

"This lady right here, Rihanna Valentine, is the animal breeder and a family friend," said Shaunabell.

Rihanna Valentine shook hands with them. "Yes, I'm the one that bred Rebel's father, a German Shepherd, with his mother, a wolf.

"That puppy was like a son to me. My doctor had recommended that I raise animals instead of getting pregnant and having my own children, because of concerns about my mental health. It has to do with what happened to my great-grandmother, but that conversation will have to wait for another time."

"Well, you really made a big difference in our lives through that puppy son of yours," said Mary." Thank you, Miss Valentine."

"How do you know that I'm not married?"

"Well, I don't see a ring on your finger."

Shaunabell stepped in to protect Rihanna's privacy. "See, look. I don't have a ring on my finger. But this hunk husband and I are madly in love with each other!" Then she kissed Simon hard on the lips.

Mark senior chuckled. Then he kissed his wife hard on the lips, too, in front of their birth son.

Mark junior, and even Rihanna, chuckled.

"All right, my four moms and dads. Let's have our Thanksgiving lunch!" said Mark junior. "You too, Rihanna. Then we will have to get ready to receive our rewards for Rebel's One-of-a-kind Miracle Blood, tonight!"

. . .

At the Lotto Max office, Constable Dave received a cheque for five million dollars. He was interviewed by the press and had to pose for photos.

When that was finished, he drove Lynnora to her bank and made sure the cheque was deposited directly in her account.

Chapter Thirty-Four

After Thanksgiving lunch was over, all the patients returned to their units to get ready for the 'Rebel's One-of-a-kind Miracle Blood Award.'

Rihanna lay down for her nap and asked herself, "What am I supposed to do next in this world? And what does 'Rebel's One-of-a-kind Miracle Blood' have to do with me?" Then she drifted off to sleep and started dreaming...

The wind was blowing through the open window. It knocked a porcelain statue of a half-wolf-and-half-German Shepherd off the table and it broke in half.

"Oh, no!" Rihanna cried in her dream. "My precious porcelain statue souvenir is broken! It meant everything to me!" Rihanna buried her face in her hands, feeling all upset. "How am I ever make it one piece again?"

Then she heard a strange voice. "I am back in one piece." Rihanna quickly turned and saw something she had never seen before in her whole life. It was a spirit standing in front of her, by the window. "Who are you?" asked Rihanna.

"I am Rebel, an angel sent by The Heavenly Creator. God loves you, because you're His child. Since your bipolar disorder was completely healed by 'Rebel's One-of-a-kind Miracle Blood', God has a mission for you.

"The whole world is in danger from dangerous German criminals who will conquer the entire world, if two valuable witnesses do not testify in court.

"The first is Barbara Royal, usually called Bubble, the employee that you fired from the hair salon who is also your third cousin.

"The other is Elaine Williams, the daughter of your third cousin, Pam Williams. Elaine has a rare disease called 'Hitler's Mania,' which will put her in a coma and kill her before she turns thirty, just as it did to your and Pam's great-grandmother.

"Your first mission is to convince Barbara to agree to a transfusion of 'Rebel's One-of-a-kind Miracle Blood.' Until she is cured of her schizophrenia, she will not be allowed to testify in the court case against the criminals.

"Your second mission is to go to Pam and convince her to save her daughter with the same kind of transfusion.

"From now on, you are on your own. But God will be guiding you every step of the way. Good luck."

...In real life Rihanna woke up from her nap when she heard a nurse calling her name.

"Rihanna? ... Rihanna?... It's time for you to get dressed up for the award tonight. We'll also be having Thanksgiving supper in the cafeteria."

"Boy, that wind really knocked down my porcelain statue onto the floor, and broke it in half," said Rihanna.

"It doesn't look broken to me," said the nurse. "It's still standing there by the window. I kept the window closed the whole time when you were sleeping. Anyway, you've got to hurry up! You don't want to be late!"

The nurse left the room.

"I must've been dreaming," Rihanna thought, but she took the dream message to heart.

Chapter Thirty-Five

The Award/Thanksgiving supper for 'Rebel's One-of-a-kind Miracle Blood' was underway in the cafeteria and there was a big crowd of patients, families and friends. As soon as everyone was seated, the host rang a small bell, to get the audience's attention.

"Good evening, everyone! Thank you for being here. My name is Dr. Brian Larry James. Without further ado, I would like to turn the microphone over to my colleague. He is the man who discovered the substance that improves quality-of-life for individuals with bipolar disorder and schizophrenia." He turned to his guest and nodded. "Please begin."

"Good evening, everyone!" said the guest speaker. "Thank you for coming to hear about my discovery.

"First, let me introduce myself. My name is Dr. Pierre Royal Mackenzie. I am a scientist and I have been working on a top-secret project.

"It all started with how the now-deceased crossbreed dog named 'Rebel' responded to stimuli. Rebel was born with a powerful mind and a powerful heart. He had mixed blood from his wolf mother and his German Shepherd father. He was the healthiest offspring and lived to be a miracle dog. He passed away thirteen years ago. Rebel was unique.

"Rebel's story is about how this strong-minded animal handled his traumatic life of abuse and neglect after his first owner, Robert, put him up for adoption at two months of age. He was seen tied up in the backyard from early morning until dark while his abusive owner was at work, according to witnesses in the neighborhood. They also reported that this vulnerable animal was frequently subjected to violence.

"They could often hear the owner yelling at the frightened dog, sometimes in the middle of the night, loud enough to keep everyone awake.

"One night, several people called the authorities. The police arrived and caught the abusive owner in the act. He was arrested on the spot and the victimized pet was taken to the SPCA.

"According to the vet's story, Rebel recovered and was returned to his original owner. The dog showed strong love and patience toward his owner and his loving girlfriend.

"The couple took Rebel with them when they went to Lake Louise for a vacation. That was where he connected with a young boy, a five-year-old that I have been working with. Rebel jumped into the water and tried to swim to the boy who was stranded on a small boat, but he wasn't experienced enough, and had to be rescued by his owner and girlfriend.

"Once they got Rebel back to shore, they realized that the dog was exhausted. They took him immediately to a vet where they explained how the brave dog, despite having no swimming experience, risked his own life to rescue the abandoned boy. According to the vet, the dog was the healthiest animal he had ever seen and would make a good role model.

"Sometime later, after returning home from their vacation, they noticed that Rebel was showing signs of slowing down. They took him to the vet again. The sad results were that this animal that was so healthy a few weeks earlier had only two days left to live."

In the cafeteria audience, Robert and his brother, Dave were feeling emotional, and had tears in their eyes. Rihanna also had a couple of tears.

The scientist continued, "The last moments of Rebel's life were very dramatic. The abusive second owner had tracked down the first owner and was holding them in the basement of a burning house and threatening to kill them all.

"Rebel went looking for help and found his owner's brother, who recognized the dog and quickly realized that he was trying to convey a message. He and his family ran to the burning house. His wife dialed 911 while he went into the basement.

"But he just ended up being another hostage. When Rebel sensed the danger, he jumped right through the glass of a basement window and attacked the man with the gun. Now, they all escaped, but afterwards, the exhausted dog lay down between the two men and died.

"Rebel was handed over to me at my lab. There, I examined the dog's blood and it turned out to be very powerful. I did a lot of research into what that blood can do for the human brain.

"One day, my partner, Dr. James, brought to us a five-year-old boy who had been adopted, and who happened to be the same boy that Rebel had tried to rescue from the boat, and asked me to see if I could find a cure for his bipolar disorder and schizophrenia. Apparently, the normal drugs weren't working well for him, and two new powerful drugs that they tried caused an allergic reaction.

"I agreed to try a transfusion with the powerful blood into the patient's body. At first, the patient slept for two weeks. When he woke up, he appeared normal, but we monitored him for another nine weeks.

"All of our tests indicated that the young patient no longer showed signs of bipolar disorder and schizophrenia. The powerful blood turned out to be a cure. This was an incredible discovery!

"Dr. James and I came up with a name for the powerful blood: 'Rebel's One-of-a-kind Miracle Blood!'

"We have been monitoring that boy ever since. We worked with his teachers, his employers and even his gym instructors, and had them send us written evaluations of how well the boy was behaving in those environments.

"It clearly showed that 'Rebel's One-of-a-kind Miracle Blood' has been keeping the young lad in reality!

"Since then, we have tested the cure on another man with schizophrenia. It turns out that this man is the one who originally rescued both the struggling brave dog and the five-year-old abandoned boy. And he is now doing well.

"This Miracle Blood is now proven to be a cure for anyone with bipolar disorder and schizophrenia!

"The donor for all of the transfusions of 'Rebel's One-of-a-kind Miracle Blood' deserves an award. He will now be a lifetime donor for all individuals with bipolar disorder and schizophrenia — Mark Barker! Come on up to the stage, Mark!"

Everyone applauded as Mark walked up to the front where the guest speaker was standing. Mark stood in front of the audience and collected his award. "Thank you, everyone! It is my honour to be a lifetime donor for 'Rebel's One-of-a-kind Miracle Blood'. Everyone deserves the improved quality-of-life that this cure can bring. Thank you."

Mark received a big round of applause as he returned to his seat with his four parents.

Next, it was Robert's turn. After he collected his award plaque he turned to the audience. "Thank you, everyone! It was my honour to be part of the experiment for this Miracle Blood! Thank you!"

Then Leo Lightheart came up to the stage. He stood in front of the audience and collected his award plaque. "Thank you, everyone! It was my privilege to be a witness in the case of the missing man who later became part of this experiment! Thank you!"

Finally, it was Rihanna's turn. Rihanna stood there in front of the audience and collected her award. "Thank you, everyone! It was my honour to be Rebel's human mother when he was born! He was my little angel! Thank you!"

"Thank you all for coming and all the best to all patients who can now receive 'Rebel's One-of-a-kind Miracle Blood'! Enjoy your Thanksgiving supper!" said the host, Dr. James.

Chapter Thirty-Six

The next day at sunset, Simon and Shaunabell were standing on the quiet highway in Lake Louise. They knelt down to pet the two angels, saying goodbye to the white blue-eyed wolf and the black German Shepherd.

The two animals turned away and began trotting down the quiet highway together. The couple stood up, watching them as they headed back to where they came from – their home in heaven. As they watched, the two blended together into a single half-wolf-and-half-German Shepherd.

The angel turned back to look at the couple for one last time and then let out a howling goodbye. Simon waved at the howling half-wolf-and-half-German Shepherd angel, while Shaunabell smiled. Then the angel continued trotting down the highway and slowly disappeared in a yellow bright light.

Simon turned to Shaunabell and kissed her. They could hear heavenly music playing from the forest, where the angel had disappeared. Then they boarded the air ambulance and flew off to their new home in Edmonton to start their new careers and be close to their son.

The End